Indigent Defenders

Get the Job Done and Done Well

Submitted to the State Justice Institute

by

National Center for State Courts

ROGER A. HANSON   BRIAN J. OSTROM
WILLIAM E. HEWITT   CHRISTOPHER LOMVARDIAS

May 1992

©1992
National Center for State Courts
Williamsburg, Virginia 23187-8798
Publication Number R-133
Library of Congress Catalog Card Number: 92-60868
ISBN 0-89656-113-5

This report was developed under a grant from the State Justice Institute, grant number SJI-89-05X-B-045. The opinions and points of view expressed in this report are those of the authors. The opinions expressed do not necessarily represent the official position or policies of the State Justice Institute.

Acknowledgments

Many individuals have helped produce this examination of indigent defense in nine courts. Judges, court staff, and attorneys, including both prosecutors and indigent defense counsel, gave generously of their time in discussing issues, resolving data collection problems, and reviewing project results. Special thanks are given to Chief Judge Dalton Roberson and Mr. George Gish, court administrator, Detroit Recorder's Court; Mr. Benjamin Blake, chief defender, Legal Aid and Defender Association of Detroit; Ms. Barbara Gletne, administrator, King County Office of Public Defense; Mr. Ronald H. Clark, chief deputy, Criminal Division of the King County Prosecuting Attorney Office; Mr. Gary Tomlinson, trial court administrator, King County Superior Court; Ms. Janet Adams, court administrator, Denver District Court; Mr. David F. Vela, Colorado public defender; Mr. Stephen M. Flavin, Colorado deputy public defender; Mr. Norman S. Early, Jr., Denver district attorney; Mr. Gary R. Wright, chief deputy clerk, Norfolk Circuit Court; Mr. John R. Doyle III, chief deputy, Office of the Commonwealth Attorney, Norfolk, Virginia; Mr. James E. Brix, assistant court administrator, Monterey County California Superior Court; Mr. D. Michael Lawrence, public defender, Monterey County; Mr. Dean D. Flippo, district attorney, Monterey County; Mr. Jeff Henthorn, superior court administrator, and Ms. Donna Howe, clerk, Oxford County Maine Superior Court; Ms. Janet T. Mills, district attorney, Auburn, Maine; John S. Jenness, Esquire, South Paris, Maine; Presiding Judge Edward L. Dawson, Judge Robert Duber, and Ms. Mary Hawkins, court administrator, Gila County Superior Court; Mr. Joseph Albo, Gila County attorney; Judges Richard L. Pitt and Alan R. Hancock, Washington Superior Court for the Counties of Island and San Juan; Ms. Jane Bradshaw, coordinator, Island County Indigent Defense Program; Ms. Mary Jean Cahail, clerk of the Superior Court for San Juan County; and Ms. Peggy Vesser, trial court administrator, Island/San Juan Superior Court.

A distinguished advisory committee composed of the Honorable Kevin S. Burke, Hennepin County Minnesota District Court; Professor George Cole, University of Connecticut; Ms. Angela Davis, director, Public Defender Service, Washington, D.C.; Honorable Thomas H. Dorwart, Nebraska County Court; Mr. Peter S. Gilchrist III, district attorney, Mecklenburg County, North Carolina; Mr. Ivar Goldart, deputy attorney-in-charge, New York Legal Aid Society; the Honorable Sanford J. Jones, Fulton County, Georgia, Juvenile Court; Mr. R. William Linden, Jr., state court administrator, Oregon; and Mr. William E. Smalley, assistant court administrator, Fulton County Georgia Superior Court. The committee members suggested numerous improvements in the interpretation of the research results and helped the project staff put the results into proper perspective.

The report also benefited from the input and advice of colleagues at the National Center for State Courts. Special thanks are extended to Ms. Joy Chapper, clerk of the District of Columbia Court of Appeals, who was previously a member of the NCSC project staff. Dr. Sally T. Hillsman, vice president of the NCSC's Research Division, also offered constructive criticisms.

Putting the manuscript into final form benefited from the independent review and editing of Mr. William Fishback and Mr. Charles Campbell. Expert design and artwork were provided by Ms. Hisako Sayers of NCSC's Publications Service.

Finally, the support of the State Justice Institute in sponsoring the research is much appreciated. In particular, the monitoring of the project by Mr. Philip W. Toelkes and Ms. Daina Farthing-Capowich brought the study to a happy conclusion. To all of these individuals and many others in the field, the project staff is uncommonly grateful.

Project Staff

ROGER A. HANSON
Project Director

WILLIAM E. HEWITT
Senior Staff Associate

BRIAN J. OSTROM
Senior Staff Associate

CHRISTOPHER LOMVARDIAS
Staff Associate

DEBORAH F. GAUSE
Administrative Secretary

Contents

Page	
iii	Acknowledgments
vii	List of Tables
1	**Chapter I:** *Indigent Defense: The Research*
3	Introduction
6	Statement of Objective
8	Organizational Road Map
9	**Chapter II:** *Structure and Context of Indigent Defense*
11	Introduction
12	What Do the Indigent Defense Systems Look Like?
16	Detroit's Indigent Defense System
18	Seattle's Indigent Defense System
21	Denver's Indigent Defense System
23	Norfolk's Indigent Defense System
24	Monterey's Indigent Defense System
25	Globe's Indigent Defense System
26	Oxford's Indigent Defense System
26	Island's Indigent Defense System
27	San Juan's Indigent Defense System
28	Context of Indigent Defense: Comparative Overview
35	Summary
37	**Chapter III:** *Timeliness*
39	Introduction
40	Length of Time from Arrest to Disposition
40	Meeting the ABA Standard
42	Upper-court-processing Time
42	The Effects of Defense Counsel on Case-processing Time
47	Summary

v

49	**Chapter IV:** *Performance and Indigent Defense*
51	Introduction
52	Conviction Rates
55	Charge Reductions
57	Incarceration Rates
60	Lengths of Prison Sentences
60	Summary
63	**Chapter V:** *Cost and Management of Indigent Defense*
65	Introduction
66	Co-optation Versus Professionalism
71	A Framework for Assessing the Cost of Indigent Defense
74	Assigned Counsel Systems
81	Public Defender Systems
89	Contract Defender Systems
92	Overall Patterns in Resource Allocation Across the Nine Courts
93	Comparing the Resources Available to the Prosecutor and Public Defender
99	Summary
101	**Chapter VI:** *Conclusions and Implications*
103	Summary
104	Indigent Defenders: A New Profession
105	Implications
107	**Appendix:** *Profiles of the Nine Research Sites: The Environments, the Courts, and the Prosecutors' Offices*

List of Tables

Table 1   Defense Representation—Structure and Institutional Issues

Table 2   What is the Percent of Different Types of Defense Attorneys in the Courts?

Table 3   What Do the Communities Look Like?

Table 4   Felony Courts—Structure, Calendaring, and Scheduling Practices

Table 5   Caseload Composition in the Courts

Table 6   Prosecution Screening, Plea Authority, and Staffing Structure

Table 7   What Is the Typical Length of Time that Indigent Defenders and Privately Retained Counsel Take to Resolve Cases?

Table 8   Do Indigent Defenders or Privately Retained Counsel More Closely Approximate the ABA's Time Standards?

Table 9   Is the Upper-court Case-processing Time for Indigent Defenders Shorter or Longer than for Privately Retained Counsel?

Table 10   Is the Type of Criminal Defense Attorney Associated with the Pace of Litigation?

Table 11   Is the Type of Criminal Defense Attorney Associated with the Pace of Litigation Controlling for the Type of Disposition?

Table 12   Is the Type of Criminal Defense Attorney Associated with the Pace of Litigation Controlling for the Type of Offense?

Table 13 Does the Type of Criminal Defense Attorney Make a Difference in the Pace of Litigation Controlling for the Type of Disposition and the Type of Offense?

Table 14 Are Defendants Represented by Indigent Defenders More Likely to Be Convicted than Defendants Represented by Privately Retained Counsel?

Table 15 At Trial, Are Privately Retained Counsel More Successful than Indigent Defenders?

Table 16 Do Privately Retained Counsel Have Lower Conviction Rates in Different Sized Courts?

Table 17 Do Privately Retained Counsel Gain More Charge Reductions than Indigent Defenders in Cases Disposed of by Guilty Pleas?

Table 18 Do Privately Retained Counsel Gain More Charge Reductions than Publicly Appointed Attorneys?

Table 19 Are Privately Retained Counsel More Successful Indigent Defenders in Keeping their Clients out of Jail or Prison?

Table 20 Is the Incarceration Rate for Privately Retained Counsel Lower than for Publicly Appointed Counsel?

Table 21 Is the Incarceration Rate Lower for Privately Retained Counsel than for Publicly Appointed Counsel in Large and Small Courts?

Table 22 Do Privately Retained Counsel Gain Shorter Prison Sentences than Indigent Defenders?

Table 23 How Much Money Is Spent on Indigent Defense?

Table 24 What Are the Resources of Assigned Counsel Systems?

Table 25 What Was the Average Full Payment to Assigned Counsel Before (1987 and 1988) and After (1989) the Introduction of the Flat Fee Schedule in Detroit?

Introduction   ix

Table 26   How Are Resources Distributed in Island County's Assigned
           Counsel System?

Table 27   What Are the Resources of Public Defender Systems?

Table 28   How Are Resources Distributed in Seattle's Three Public
           Defender Firms?

Table 29   How Are Resources Distributed in Denver's Public Defender's
           Office?

Table 30   How Are Resources Distributed in Monterey's Public Defender's
           Office?

Table 31   How Are Resources Distributed in Detroit's Legal Aid and
           Defender Association Office?

Table 32   What Are the Resources of Contract Attorney Systems?

Table 33   How Do the Resources of the Prosecutor Compare to the Indigent
           Defense Offices in Seattle, Denver, and Monterey?

Table 34   What Is the Availability of Expert Witnesses, Training,
           and Libraries?

Table 35   Comparison of Prosecution and Indigent Defense in Detroit, 1989

Chapter I
Indigent Defense: The Research

Indigent Defense: The Research

Introduction

The emergence and growth of professional criminal defense attorneys for indigent defendants are among the most important contemporary developments in the American legal system. That conclusion is the overarching observation drawn from a study of nine state trial courts of general jurisdiction conducted by researchers from the National Center for State Courts (NCSC). The NCSC study team reached that conclusion based on the following empirical results concerning the dispositions of felony cases in the courts studied.

(1) Indigent defenders dispose of their cases in a relatively speedy manner. The time that they take to resolve their cases comes closer to the American Bar Association's Time Standards than does the time taken in cases handled by privately retained defense counsel.

(2) Indigent defenders achieve timeliness without sacrificing the interests of defendants. They are as successful as privately retained counsel in gaining favorable outcomes for their clients (e.g., acquittals, charge reductions, and short sentences to prison).

(3) The success of indigent defenders in resolving cases expeditiously and favorably for their clients is not limited to particular courts or to particular types of indigent defense systems (e.g., public defender versus assigned counsel or contract attorneys). They do well vis-à-vis privately retained attorneys whether the data are combined or considered separately according to the methods by which defense attorneys gain appointments.

(4) The success of indigent defenders is attributable, at least in part, to the presence of experienced counsel among public defenders, assigned counsel, and contract attorneys. The experience of indigent defenders is evident when it is compared to that of prosecutors.

(5) There is a close approximation of parity between public defenders and prosecutors in the areas of compensation, training, and staff support and to a lesser degree in the areas of expert witnesses and investigators.

These results gain significance in light of the long-standing and sharp criticisms of indigent defenders in the literature. Indigent defenders have been characterized as marginal in performance, ill equipped, and poorly trained since the classic studies of the administration of justice that were undertaken in the 1920s. Roscoe

Pound, who is one of the founding fathers of the field, made the following comment on the nature of criminal defense counsel in Cleveland:

> Want of education, want of organization, want of discipline of those who are habitually most active in defending accused persons in our large cities, are conspicuous and significant facts.[1]

Certainly Pound did not want of opinions. However, one might think that contemporary critics are more restrained. After all, a reasonable expectation is that indigent defense work improved with the United States Supreme Court's decisions that defendants have a fundamental right to the assistance of counsel.[2] Consistent with those declarations, the Court ordered state and local governments to establish and to finance systems of appointed attorneys. Although indigent defense was not a constitutional matter in Pound's lifetime, today's critics are just as trenchant in their views of indigent defenders. Moreover, current skeptics do not limit their judgments to backwater areas, as evidenced by the following view of McConville and Mirsky concerning New York City's appointed counsel arrangement:

> Against this background, the creation of an indigent defense system whose object is the mass disposal of criminal cases through guilty pleas, lesser pleas, and other non-trial dispositions should not be viewed as a heroic response to the needs of poor people by public-spirited individuals. Nor should it be viewed as a rational response to modern case pressure, as a product of the individual, or collective behavior of courtroom actors, or as the logical result of procedural and evidential complexity attendant upon a trial. Instead, the routine processing of defendants is exactly what the indigent defense system was designed to accomplish.[3]

McConville and Mirsky make the strong claim that New York City's problems are representative of all communities across the country.[4] They contend that New York is a "microcosm" of the nation's indigent defense system. To the extent that

---

[1] Pound, *Criminal Justice and the American City*, in Criminal Justice in Cleveland 636 (R. Pound and F. Frankfurter eds. 1968).

[2] Gideon v. Wainwright, 372 U.S. 335 (1963); Argersinger v. Hamlin, 407 U.S. 25 (1972); Scott v. Illinois, 440 U.S. 367 (1979).

[3] McConville & Mirsky, *Criminal Defense of the Poor in New York City*, 15 New York University Review of Law and Social Change 582, at 881-83 (1986-87).

[4] An underlying theme to McConville and Mirsky's work is that indigent defenders are co-opted by the courthouse community. This theme is a traditional one in the literature. *See, e.g.*, Sudnow, *Normal Crimes: A Sociological Feature of the Penal Code in a Public Defender Office*, 12 Social Problems 253 (1965);

the nine courts in the current study capture the contextual variation that exists across the country, this research provides the opportunity to test the scope of McConville and Mirsky's claim.

In addition to the observers who criticize indigent defenders for alleged incompetence, there is another line of criticism that says they are of limited influence in shaping what goes on in criminal courts. This claim asserts that a lack of an electoral base puts defense attorneys in a weak position. This criticism is represented by the views of Nardulli, Eisenstein, and Flemming. They write:

> Even under the best conditions an analysis of the structure of the local defense bar would yield few insights into the overall orientation toward work within a court community. Much of the work is done by solo practitioners and is characterized by idiosyncratic strategies and tactics adopted (sic) to the local terrain. The contours of that terrain are determined by the mix of judicial and prosecutorial practices and policies just reviewed. Defense work is reactive because, with few exceptions, attorneys can have little impact upon the shape of this terrain. Even the head of the public defender's office, if one exists, does not enjoy the clout of his or her counterparts. He or she is not likely to be a powerful or respected elected official but rather someone who depends upon someone else for both appointment and tenure, as well as budget. Neither does the head public defender exercise control over key aspects of the dispositional process such as charging, case scheduling, and sentencing. But, despite the relative impotence of the defense bar in landscaping the terrain, they are active players on it. No analysis of the court community's infrastructure can be complete without a review of the defense bar.[5]

Are the critics correct or incorrect in their generalizations? Unfortunately, the answer is not obvious. There are several reasons for taking another look at this topic due to the inherent limitations in past research.

Basically, prior studies have three deficiencies. First, many of the studies fail to go beyond the boundaries of a single court and thereby lack comparative perspective.[6] Second, cross-court studies tend not to incorporate large, medium, and small

---

Blumberg, *The Practice of Law Is a Confidence Game: Organizational Co-optation of a Profession*, 1 Law and Society Review 15 (1967); Eckart & Stover, *Public Defenders and Routinized Criminal Defense Processes*, 51 Journal of Urban Law 665 (May 1974); Levine, *The Impact of "Gideon": The Performance of Public and Private Criminal Defense Lawyers*, 8 Polity 215 (1975); I. Balbus, The Dialectics of Legal Repression (1973); Mounts & Wilson, *Systems for Providing Indigent Defense: An Introduction*, 14 New York University Review of Law and Social Change 193 (1986); G. Cole, The American System of Criminal Justice (1992).

[5] P. Nardulli, J. Eisenstein, & R. Flemming, The Tenor of Justice: Criminal Courts and the Guilty Plea Process 190-91 (1988).

[6] *See, e.g.*, L. McIntyre, The Public Defender: The Practice of Law in the Shadows of Repute (1987).

communities,[7] thus failing to control for the effects of population size, which generally are regarded as influential in shaping the delivery of most public services. Third, none of the prior studies compare all of the basic types of defenders (e.g., public defender, assigned counsel, and contract attorneys) to privately retained counsel.[8] As a result, available evaluations of indigent defense performance are incomplete.

Statement of Objective

The objective of this report is to describe the knowledge gained from an examination of felony dispositions in nine state general jurisdiction trial courts and the role that indigent defenders play in their respective systems. The research addressed a series of interrelated issues that are central to understanding the effects that indigent defenders have both on court operations and on defendants. Do indigent defenders frustrate or promote the court's desire to dispose of cases expeditiously? Do indigent defenders rush their clients to guilty pleas? When they go to trial, how frequently do they win acquittals? How is the money for indigent defense services spent and managed? Do the budgetary allocations for indigent defenders look different than the prosecutor's allocations? Where do the similarities and differences between the two allocations lie?

The answers to these questions are drawn from an examination of felony case processing in the following nine diverse courts: (1) Wayne County (Detroit, Michigan) Circuit Court; (2) King County (Seattle, Washington) Superior Court; (3) Denver County (Colorado) District Court; (4) Norfolk (Virginia) Circuit Court; (5) Monterey County (Salinas, California) Superior Court; (6) Oxford County (South Paris, Maine) Superior Court; (7) Gila County (Globe, Arizona) Superior Court; (8) Island County

---

[7] Some studies, for example, focus exclusively on very large communities. See, for example, Robert Hermann, Eric Single, and John Boston's study of New York, Los Angeles, and Washington, D.C., Counsel for the Poor: Criminal Defense in Urban America (1977). See also James Eisenstein and Herbert Jacob's study of Baltimore, Detroit, and Chicago in Felony Justice: An Organizational Analysis of Criminal Courts (1977). On the other hand, Peter Nardulli focuses exclusively on nine medium-sized communities (DuPage, Peoria, and St. Clair counties, Illinois; Kalamazoo, Oakland, and Saginaw counties, Michigan; Dauphin, Erie, and Montgomery counties, Pennsylvania) in *Insider's Justice: Defense Attorneys and the Handling of Felony Cases*, 77 Journal of Criminal Law and Criminology 379 (1986). Prior research with the broadest scope is a study of eight medium-sized and small-sized communities all located in Virginia by Larry J. Cohen, Patricia P. Semple, Robert E. Crew, Jr., *Assigned Counsel Versus Public Defender Systems in Virginia: A Comparison of Relative Benefits*, in The Defense Counsel (W. F. McDonald ed. 1983).

[8] Some of the studies, in fact, do not compare indigent defenders to privately retained counsel. See, for example, M. McConville & C. Mirsky, Criminal Defense of the Poor in New York City (1986-87). The lack of a comparison group poses severe methodological problems because evaluations require some form of comparison.

(Coupeville, Washington) Superior Court; and (9) San Juan County (Friday Harbor, Washington) Superior Court.[9]

The nine communities were chosen to satisfy five criteria. First, the nine courts were chosen from 39 large and 10 small-sized communities that the NCSC had studied previously to enhance the existing knowledge concerning those courts and to minimize the cost of additional data collection.[10] The previous studies provided some data (e.g., case-processing times) based on random samples of felony cases disposed of in 1987. It was believed that additional information (e.g., sentences) could be gathered efficiently without having to draw entirely new samples. Second, the large-sized courts were chosen because they indicated that the chief variable—the type of defense counsel—could be identified for each case in the sample of 1987 dispositions from their automated management information systems. Some of the 39 large-sized courts indicated that this piece of information was unavailable or inaccessible and, therefore, they were not considered further. This criterion was not a factor in the small-sized courts because none of the 10 potential sites had automated systems. As it turned out, the reliance on existing databases was less efficient than anticipated. Case files in all of the courts had to be reexamined because of missing, incomplete, or incorrect data. Third, the cooperation of the court, prosecutor, and defense counsel was necessary. Some of the potential sites indicated no interest in participating in the study during exploratory discussions. For this reason, the communities of Island and San Juan were included despite the need for entirely original data collection. Fourth, the State Justice Institute suggested the importance of having contract systems in both the large- and small-sized courts. Whereas this consideration did not exclude any community, it did give priority to particular communities. Fifth, the remaining sites were chosen to provide a balance of geographic, economic, social, and cultural diversity. Thus, while the nine courts that were selected are not necessarily representative of all courts, they do represent a broad spectrum along which many courts in the country can be located.

Case-related information was obtained from random samples of felony cases disposed of in 1987. As a result, this report provides a description of the courts in 1987 except where explicit references are made to other years. The analysis of case-related data was augmented with interviews of approximately 125 defense attorneys,

---

[9] Hereafter, the courts will be referred to as Detroit, Seattle, Denver, Norfolk, Monterey, Oxford, Globe, Island, and San Juan.

[10] Detroit, Seattle, Denver, Norfolk, and Monterey were part of an NCSC examination of criminal case-processing time in 39 urban courts, see J. Goerdt, C. Lomvardias, & G. Gallas, Reexamining the Pace of Litigation in 39 Urban Trial Courts (1991). Globe and Oxford were part of a parallel study in ten rural courts, see Miller, *Delay in the Rural Courts: It Exists, but It Can Be Reduced*, 14 State Court Journal (Summer 1990).

prosecutors, judges, and court staff across the nine courts. Additional data on the cost of indigent defense and prosecutors' offices were collected for the period 1987-89.

Organizational Road Map

The remaining portion of this report is devoted to reporting the results of the inquiry into the nine courts. Chapter II offers an overview of the indigent defense system in each court and its context. In Chapter III, the timeliness with which indigent defenders resolve their cases is addressed for each court and for all of the courts grouped together. Chapter IV is an analysis of case outcomes for the defendants and whether indigent defenders gain favorable results for their clients. Chapter V offers a description of the allocation and management of indigent defense resources. Finally, in Chapter VI, overall conclusions are drawn and the policy implications of the data are put forth for consideration.

Chapter II
Structure and Context of Indigent Defense

Structure and Context of Indigent Defense

Introduction

The purposes of this chapter are fourfold: first, the objective is to describe the indigent defense system in each of the nine courts. What is the basic structure in each court? How is the match made between attorneys and indigent defendants? What types of experience do indigent defenders have? Second, the chapter provides an overview of the communities surrounding each court. An understanding of the social and economic environments is important because these may affect indigent defense performance. For example, do indigent defenders perform well in large-sized communities but less well in small-sized communities? Third, the aim is to highlight essential aspects of the court system in which the indigent defenders practice. The final objective is to examine the other organization with which indigent defenders regularly interact; namely, the prosecutor's office.

These objectives are addressed in terms of available statistics and the results of systematic interviews with key participants. The discussion is organized in four ways. First, the systems of indigent defense are introduced and summarized. Second, each court's indigent defense system is examined. The third portion of the chapter is a comparative overview of the communities, the courts, and the prosecutors' offices. The overview describes the similarities and differences among the nine courts and provides the reader with a framework for understanding the complexities of each individual court.[11] Finally, a summary to the chapter integrates the overviews and the individual indigent defense system descriptions and anticipates lessons that will emerge in the analysis of the data despte their being obscured by the variety found among the indigent defense systems in the nine courts. For example, why should all "public defender" services be thought to be alike? Is the key to improving indigent services only to be found in altering the structure that is used, or can a given structure be adapted to meet particular conditions and problems more effectively? What characteristics, if any, cut across different types of systems? How do some systems organize themselves to avoid potential pitfalls?

---

[11] The overview is drawn from data that are, for expository reasons, placed in an appendix. Those readers who seek nuance and color in detailed case studies will find satisfaction in the appendix.

11

What Do the Indigent Defense Systems Look Like?

Legal representation of indigent defendants is viewed commonly as fitting into one of three basic categories: (1) public defender, (2) assigned counsel, and (3) contract attorneys. The conventional wisdom is that each category has a particular organizational structure, a particular method of financing, and an orientation toward achieving one or more of several different goals, such as efficiency, accountability, or effectiveness. Moreover, systems in each category are presumed to be alike (e.g., all public defender offices are similar).[12]

One or more of these three basic categories is represented in each of the nine courts. If the courts are classified according to the major provider of services, as seen in **Table 1**, then Seattle, Denver, and Monterey are public defender systems; Detroit, Norfolk, Oxford, and Island are assigned counsel systems; and Globe and San Juan are contract systems.

This configuration corresponds to the expected pattern of public defender offices existing primarily in large communities and rarely, if at all, in small communities. The occurrence of assigned counsel systems in four of the nine courts is consistent with the national pattern of assigned counsel systems being the most common type of system. And the two contract systems in Globe and in San Juan fit the national estimate that this type of system exists in a minority of usually small-sized courts,[13] including both those involving indigent defendants and those involving nonindigent defendants.

Table 2 indicates the proportion of felony dispositions in 1987 drawn from random samples of case files that were represented by public defenders, assigned counsel, contract attorneys, and privately retained counsel in each of the nine courts. (There were no instances of unrepresented defendants in any of the nine courts.) The volume of cases represented by privately retained counsel is 20 percent or more in five of the courts (Denver, Norfolk, Oxford, Island, and San Juan), and it is nearly that large in Globe (18 percent) and in Detroit (17.1 percent). Despite assertions to the contrary by some observers,[14] therefore, the evidence from the nine courts indicates that the private defense bar is not an endangered species, unless privately retained counsel are expected to handle a majority of the cases in order to be deemed viable.[15]

---

[12] *See, e.g.*, D. Neubauer, America's Courts and the Criminal Justice System (1988).

[13] R. Spangenberg, B. Lee, M. Battaglia, P. Smith, & A. D. Davis, National Criminal Defense System Study: Final Report (U.S. Department of Justice 1986).

[14] P. Wice, Criminal Lawyers: An Endangered Species (1978).

[15] There are minor differences in the caseload composition of defense attorneys. All three basic categories of indigent defenders tend to have the same distribution of felony cases. Most of their cases involve burglary and theft offenses followed by, in descending order of frequency, crimes against the person, drug sale and possession, and other types of felonies. The only difference between their caseloads and those of privately retained counsel is that privately retained counsel handle more cases involving crimes against the person than burglary and theft cases. However, this difference is not sharp. As indicated by a very low correlation (Cramer's V = .16) between the type of attorney and the type of cases handled.

Table 1
Defense Representation—Structure and Institutional Issues

	Detroit	Seattle	Denver	Norfolk	Monterey	Globe	Oxford	San Juan and Island
Percent of All Felony Dispositions Handled by Indigent Defenders	83	88	80	71	90	82	53	SJ: 61 I: 66
Type(s) of Indigent Defense Structures	Assigned Counsel, Public Defender	Three Public Defender Firms on Contract, Assigned Counsel	Public Defender, Assigned Counsel, Contract Attorneys	Assigned Counsel	Public Defender, Contract Attorney, Assigned Counsel	Contract Attorney, Assigned Counsel	Assigned Counsel	Contract Attorney, Assigned Counsel
Source of Funding	County	County	State	State	County	County	State	County
Eligibility of Attorneys for Appointment	Certification by Court; Judge Appoints to Case at First Appearance	Private Assignment Rare and Handled Informally	Pre-1990, No Formal Requirements and Handled Informally by Judge at First Appearance	Attorney Requests to be Added to List; No Formal Requirements	No Formal Requirements on Rare Occasions When Individual Attorney Assigned	Not Applicable	Informal by Judge or Clerk	SJ: N/A I: Must be Approved by Defender Association
Average Attorney Tenure	3-6 Years (LACA)	3-5 Years	6-7 Years	Not Available	5-8 Years	15-18 Years	10-12 Years	SJ: 3 Years (1989) I: 3-8 Years

Table 2
What is the Percent of Different Types of Defense Attorneys in the Courts?
Felony Dispositions, 1987

Type of Defense Attorney	Detroit	Seattle	Denver	Norfolk	Monterey	Globe	Oxford	Island	San Juan
Public Defender	18.4% (84)	86.8% (526)	74.6% (276)	0.0 (0)	72.8% (297)	0.0 (0)	0.0 (0)	0.0 (0)	0.0 (0)
Assigned Counsel	64.6% (295)	1.2% (7)	5.4% (20)	71.1% (329)	3.7% (15)	0.0 (0)	52.9% (118)	65.6% (82)	0.0 (0)
Contract Attorney	0.0 (0)	0.0 (0)	0.0 (0)	0.0 (0)	13.5% (55)	82.4% (140)	0.0 (0)	0.0 (0)	61.3% (19)
Private Counsel	17.1% (78)	12.0% (73)	20.0% (74)	28.9% (134)	10.0% (41)	17.6% (30)	47.1% (105)	34.4% (43)	38.7% (12)
Totals	100.1% (457)	100% (606)	100% (370)	100% (463)	100% (408)	100% (170)	100% (223)	100% (125)	100% (31)

These data also provide a background against which to reconsider the conventional wisdom that indigent defender systems fall into three mutually exclusive categories (public defender, assigned counsel, and contract attorney). The experiences of the nine courts suggest that there is considerable flexibility in constructing the elements of an indigent defense system. For example, it is neither necessary nor true that the public defender's office must be the major provider of legal services if it is to be used. Detroit's Legal Aid and Defender Association, which handles 25 percent of the appointments, is a counterexample to that proposition. Additionally, all three types of indigent defense structures may be integrated into a single system as illustrated by Monterey's use of public defenders, contact attorneys, and assigned counsel. Finally, the data from the nine courts do not support the notion that a particular type of defender must exist in a particular size of community (e.g., public defenders in a large-sized community). Again, Detroit, where the dominant category is assigned counsel, is a strong counterexample to that notion. The only linkage between the categories of indigent defenders and size in the courts studied is the absence of public defenders in the four small-sized communities. But even this remnant of the conventional wisdom unravels on closer examination. Island County's system of assigned counsel exhibits several characteristics of a public defender office.

A second issue is that there are variants within each type of indigent defense category that depend on the role that each one plays in the larger system of criminal defense. The nine courts suggest, for example, that assigned counsel will be structured and managed differently when they are the primary provider than when they are a limited provider. The management of assigned counsel in Detroit[16] and the structured appointment process in Norfolk[17] where assigned counsel represent 65 and 71 percent of indigent defendants, respectively, illustrate the first portion of that proposition. Moreover, the contrast between these courts and the relatively limited attention given to assigned counsel in Denver and Monterey where they represent 5 and 7 percent of indigent defendants, respectively, illustrates the second portion of the proposition.

The variation within each category also is exemplified in three ways by the public defender offices in Seattle, Denver, Monterey, and Detroit. First, whereas public defenders are thought of as being financed by annual state or local government appropriations in roughly the same manner as other public agencies, only Denver and Monterey fit this classical model. Seattle is one exception to this traditional expectation of how public defenders are funded because the public defenders in that court operate within the framework of three private, nonprofit organizations, although each firm contracts for a given amount of money each year with the King County Office of Public Defense. Detroit is another exception to the conventional notion that public defenders operate with a budgetary allocation from the state or local executive branch. The Legal Aid and Defender Association (LADA) in Detroit demonstrates that not all public defenders operate with a fixed budget. LADA is financed through a voucher system in the same manner as are assigned counsel, who are the major providers of indigent defense services in Detroit.

Second, Detroit and Denver demonstrate that all public defender systems do not have incentives to avoid accepting court appointments. An attorney under any system may decline an appointment on the grounds that representation of the defendant would possibly conflict with the duty to represent another defendant. When this situation, generally called a conflict case, arises, the court usually recognizes the attorney's claim and appoints another attorney on an assigned counsel basis. McConville and Mirsky contend that public defender organizations have a perverse incentive to declare conflicts where they do not exist.[18] By limiting their caseloads in this manner, the public defenders can operate more comfortably within

---

[16] In Detroit, the administrative office of the court has been instrumental in introducing a management information system that tracks the appointment of cases by individual judges to individual attorneys, the disposition of cases, and the payments made to attorneys in individual cases. The court also has an extensive certification process for attorneys before they are appointed. And there is an extensive training program of seminars on emerging issues (e.g., how to defend the battered spouse who fights back), educational tapes, and a library financed by a 1 percent surcharge on vouchers.

[17] In Norfolk, possible favoritism is taken out of the appointment process by the random allocation of attorneys to particular days. Unless unusual circumstances arise, attorneys receive cases on days assigned to them. Moreover, virtually all attorneys in private practice will be on the list. Hence, there should be neither bias in making appointments nor the opportunity for marginally competent counsel to rely on court appointments.

[18] McConville & Mirsky, *Criminal Defense of the Poor in New York City*, 15 New York University Review of Law and Social Change 582, at 793-817 (1986-87).

their budgets. McConville and Mirsky call this phenomenon "case shedding." However, this situation, which McConville and Mirsky believe exists in New York City, is not inevitable. In Detroit, the voucher system of payment to all publicly appointed defense counsel means that LADA receives more money, the more cases it accepts. Therefore, no incentive to shed cases exists. In Denver, the public defender's office has control over the budget that is used to pay for assigned counsel, which means there might be an incentive to declare a minimal number of conflicts. The public defender reported that intangible credit with the Colorado Assembly is earned by returning a portion of the conflict budget at the end of the year. In contrast, in Monterey, there is no parallel mechanism to control the number of conflicts as there is in Detroit and Denver. An observable consequence is that the percent of indigency cases handled by the public defender in Monterey is less than it is in Denver. However, this difference illustrates the point that not all public defender offices are alike and that they do not all respond in the same way to common problems.

A third issue that belies the belief of hard differences between structures is that there are experienced attorneys working under every system. Experience means a knowledge of the law, court procedure, and what constitutes the key factors in winning a case. Hence, the availability of experienced attorneys with specialized knowledge helps to explain why courts have been able to use a variety of different configurations of indigent defense.

Finally, the presence of experienced defense counsel in the nine courts, as measured by average attorney tenure in Table 1, is consistent with the observations made by other researchers. McIntyre, for example, measures experience in terms of the length of time attorneys in Chicago spend in their first job in order to address the question of whether public defenders stay on the job longer than other lawyers. She finds that the average tenure for new public defenders in Chicago exceeds that of legal practitioners engaged in six other areas of practice (solo practice, house counsel, other government practice, large-sized firm, medium-sized firm, and small-sized firm). Forty-five percent of new public defenders are still in the public defender's office after five years of experience, and 28 percent are still there after 10 years.[19]

Detroit's Indigent Defense System

Detroit uses primarily assigned counsel for indigent defense. The assignments, however, are distributed between two major groups. Approximately 75 percent of the caseload is assigned by judges to individual private attorneys, with the remaining 25 percent going to the Legal Aid and Defender Association. LADA is essentially a public defender's office but without the usual publicly provided budget and management.

---

[19] L. McIntyre, The Public Defender: The Practice of Law in the Shadows of Repute 81-85 (1987).

It is a private, nonprofit defender organization that was established in 1968. The caseload division is the result of a 1972 Michigan Supreme Court order that mandated 25 percent of all criminal cases go to LADA. The director of LADA monitors this allocation very closely and ensures that it is met.

All indigent defenders, both assigned counsel and LADA attorneys, operate under the voucher system. The Wayne County payment system for assigned counsel underwent substantial change in 1988. Before July 1, 1988, attorneys were paid on an event-based schedule. They were paid separately for every court event (i.e., each hearing, motion, trial day, and so forth) based upon the seriousness of the offense. Now attorneys are paid a fixed fee based on the statutory maximum penalty for the offense (ranging from low of $475 for a 24-month maximum case to $1,400 for first-degree murder).

Assigned Counsel

To become eligible to act as appointed counsel, an attorney must complete an application form stating professional experience, criminal trial experience, and training and enroll in the Criminal Advocacy Program.[20] Before acceptance, each applicant must be favorably reviewed by a judicial standing committee composed of five judges (two selected by the chief judge of Detroit Recorder's Court, one by the chief judge of Wayne County Circuit Court, and two on the recommendation of the recorder's court bar association).

There are currently about 653 individual private attorneys on the assigned counsel list, with about 10 new attorneys being added each month and an indeterminate number (less than 10) dropping off the roll or moving to a more occasional status. This total is composed of approximately 200 hard-core "regulars," who depend on the assigned counsel system for a substantial share of their clients and income, and about 450 "irregulars," who use the assigned counsel system to supplement their private (criminal and/or civil) practice.

Each private attorney must cover his or her own overhead. However, there is money available for investigators and expert witnesses. The private attorney independently contacts an investigator, and when finished, the investigator submits

---

[20] Wayne County implemented its own Criminal Advocacy Program (CAP) in 1983. Its purpose is to "develop, expand, and maintain high professional standards of representation in felony cases." The individual sessions are designed based on input from the local bench, bar, and police and reflect issues directly applicable to practice in Wayne County. Examples of current programs are seminars on evidence, new rules of criminal procedure, handling of juvenile offenders, representation of women who fight back, and new developments in scientific evidence. For this reason, people seem to prefer it to the more general CLE classes. There is a strong incentive to attend in that the certification process to practice as assigned counsel in Wayne County requires that a certain number of these sessions be attended. Those admitted to the bar prior to 1986 must attend 6 of 11 sessions, and those admitted afterward must attend 8 of the 11 sessions. To obtain credit, an attorney must sign in when entering and complete and turn in an attendance documentation form at the end. Meeting the attendance requirements for CAP sessions is mandatory for all private-assigned and LADA attorneys. CAP is funded through a 1 percent charge on all vouchers.

a voucher to the administrative office of the court. Investigator payments have a ceiling of $150 per case.

Legal Aid and Defender Association (LADA)

There are 19 defense attorneys (in addition to the director and deputy director) who work for the Legal Aid and Defender Association. Other staff include 5 investigators, 8 clerks and administrative assistants, 4 secretaries, 1 research assistant (who also runs the library), and 1 psychologist. LADA attempts to handle all cases vertically, i. e., the same attorney handles a case from assignment to final disposition.

It appears that 25 percent of indigent defense cases are assigned to LADA— indicating compliance with the Supreme Court order. The office has virtually no automation so that all case assignment and case-tracking/management reports are done by hand. The capital punishment cases are assigned by either the director or the deputy director based on ability to handle the case. The noncapital punishment cases are assigned based on work load. An "availability sheet" lists all attorneys, the number of open cases each is handling (distinguishing between capital and noncapital cases), and the number of cases completed but awaiting sentencing. At any one time, each LADA attorney has 30 to 35 open cases. The average breakdown for a senior LADA attorney in April 1990 was 2 homicides, 4 other capital cases, 20 open noncapital cases, and 10 cases ready for sentencing.

Although LADA is often referred to as a public defender, its structure is closer to an assigned counsel/public defender hybrid. As with a public defender, LADA is overseen by an independent board, with no formal government connection, that chooses the office head and sets general policy. However, LADA attorneys generate fees in the same way as private assigned counsel (vouchers are submitted to the administrative office of the court and payments are calculated on the same scale), and this accounts for most of LADA's funding. Finally, LADA attorneys have no overhead to pay and have access to good secretarial support and experienced in-house investigators. The average tenure of attorneys at LADA is three to six years.

Seattle's Indigent Defense System

The provision of indigent defense services is overseen by the King County Office of Public Defense (OPD). The OPD contracts with three nonprofit public defender firms to provide the majority of defense representation for persons charged with felony offenses.[21] Each of the defender firms has its own board of directors and

---

[21] Several years ago, the Seattle city council, members of the bar, and some indigent defendants questioned whether there was insufficient minority representation on the boards of directors and in management positions at TDA, ACA, and SCRAP. The response, in addition to increasing the awareness of affirmative action in the three agencies, was to create a fourth firm with minority group management, Northwest Defenders Association (NDA). NDA, which did not represent felony cases at the time of this study, is not investigated.

internal management structure. The oldest and largest of the three firms is The Defender Association (TDA). In 1990-91, TDA was scheduled to handle approximately 41 percent of the felonies, 25 percent of the misdemeanors, 33 percent of the juvenile offender cases, 40 percent of the juvenile dependency, 100 percent of the involuntary commitments, and 43 percent of the cases in the Seattle municipal court. The second largest firm is the Associated Counsel for the Accused (ACA), which was assigned 37 percent of the felonies, 50 percent of the misdemeanors, 22 percent of the juvenile offender cases, and 34 percent of the cases in the Seattle municipal court. The third firm, the Society of Counsel Representing Accused Persons (SCRAP), was allocated 22 percent of the felonies, 25 percent of the misdemeanors, 33 percent of the juvenile offender cases, and 60 percent of the juvenile dependency cases.

Office of Public Defense

OPD is a division within the King County Department of Human Services, which oversees the indigent defense budget and services and assigns all indigent clients to the contracting public defender firms.[22] OPD staff completes a two-page form during a defendant interview. The form covers various aspects of the charged offense, whether an interpreter is needed, and the defendant's financial situation. Individuals are determined to be indigent if their total resources are less than 125 percent of the poverty line or if they are on public assistance.

OPD schedules monthly meetings with the heads of the defender firm to discuss issues affecting the courts. For example, recent issues included improvement of court facilities and jail overcrowding. OPD represents the defenders when defender concerns and policy issues are brought to the county council, the prosecutor, and the courts. Without the monthly meeting, consultations among the three defender firms would likely be extremely infrequent. OPD also sought to institute regular meetings with each firm's board of directors. The superior court has no regular direct liaison with indigent defense firms.

OPD assigns each case to a particular defender firm the same day as indigency is determined. Notice of the case (defendant name, charge, and bail status) is delivered to the defender firm the following day. All payments to each defender firm are specified in the contract except payments for aggravated homicide and complex fraud cases. The payment in these cases is based upon negotiation between OPD and the defender firm. The defense firms are paid monthly though OPD.[23]

---

[22] If a firm discovers a conflict, OPD reassigns the case to a nonconflicting firm. In the rare instance of a conflict across all public defender firms, the case is handled by individual assigned counsel.

[23] The defender firms have no funding in their own budgets for expert witnesses. Funds for experts are found in the superior court budget, and defenders obtain them through an order from the judge. The judge is able to sign off for up to $350. If a higher amount is requested, it goes to an audit committee for acceptance/rejection. Some of the attorneys who were interviewed were not aware of the procedure for obtaining in excess of $350.

The Defender Association (TDA)

The Defender Association, an outgrowth of Seattle's Model City Program, was created in 1969 with a staff of five. In 1987, 166 individuals were employed at TDA, 71 of whom were attorneys. It was the only agency that provided indigent defense services for all case types: felony, misdemeanor, juvenile offender, juvenile dependency, involuntary commitment, and municipal court cases.

Most new attorneys (estimated 70 percent) are recent law graduates, approximately one-third of whom participate in TDA's legal internship program before they are hired. The remaining 30 percent are typically lateral hires, often from other defense firms. The legal intern program hires law students during the summer between their second and third years of law school. They typically work in the misdemeanor division and have a caseload under direct supervision. The student has a chance to learn the TDA system, to gain a feel for the work load, and to try cases. Students are encouraged to remain during their final year in law school, and some are offered positions following graduation. There is an initial washout of attorneys at the six-month to one-year range after they discover the physical and emotional commitments required of the job. If they clear this hurdle, the average tenure is about three to five years.

Case opening and the assignment of felony cases are handled by a docket clerk overseen by the supervisor of the felony division. Cases are assigned to attorneys randomly, except for homicides, which are allocated to a small number of the most experienced attorneys. TDA experimented with a specialized drug unit (three full-time attorneys). It was anticipated that this division of labor would reduce the volume of drug cases going to all attorneys, while allowing the unit to become particularly efficient and effective. It was disbanded after a short period because the attorneys were becoming burned out and less creative.

Associated Counsel for the Accused (ACA)

In 1987 ACA employed 83 individuals, 55 of whom were attorneys. The types of cases handled by ACA are felony, misdemeanor, juvenile offender, and Seattle municipal court cases. The director of ACA values having a core of experienced attorneys (i.e., four to six years), but he has reservations about "lifers." About 20 percent of the attorneys have five to seven years' experience, and most attorneys have about three years' experience.

A satellite office just outside of Seattle in Burien handles exclusively misdemeanors and is used as a training point for new attorneys. It provides a smaller work environment (fewer judges) and an opportunity to work closely with more-experienced attorneys. Twice a year ACA has a training program patterned after national trial advocacy programs. There is also a "Totally Tuesday" lecture series—every other Tuesday on subjects of interest.

When the case information arrives from OPD, one of two office coordinators enters it into the computerized case management system. This system then generates a client contact letter, a notice of appearance, which is sent to the court, and a request for discovery, which is sent to the prosecutor. The coordinator makes a tentative assignment based on the existing work load and experience of the individual attorneys. All case assignments are reviewed by the supervisor of the criminal division.

The felony attorneys meet formally once a week to discuss all aspects of their caseloads. The 23 felony attorneys are divided into two groups, each with a supervisor, and each group meets separately once a week.

There is a rank of *senior attorney,* and those individuals take on some training responsibilities. As the office increased in size it needed and could support a more formal training component, an issue that was being addressed in 1990.

Society of Counsel Representing Accused Persons (SCRAP)

In 1987 SCRAP employed 29.5 full-time equivalents, 18 of whom were attorneys. Most attorneys are recent law school graduates. New attorneys start in juvenile offender or dependency and may work into felonies if they are interested. Most felony attorneys gain experience within the firm in other divisions, but there are some lateral hires of experienced felony lawyers. Felony attorneys are hired by an ad hoc, two-member hiring committee consisting of the felony supervisor and another felony lawyer. Tenure in the felony division was difficult to assess because the firm has only recently begun handling this type of case.

The training program is on-the-job, collegial, and informal. When attorneys join the felony unit, they are assigned a "buddy" on the staff to assist them in case preparation. When a lawyer needs coverage, he or she asks the buddy first. There is a coordinator for case assignments and a senior trial deputy with a reduced caseload. Much of the orientation process comes from the attorneys doing "a lot of hanging out" and discussing their cases.

The felony unit meets to discuss defense options and strategies. Every other week is devoted to a "substantive area" (e.g., understanding DUI laws). A weekend or weeklong retreat for staff was in development. Finally, attendance at continuing legal education programs is encouraged.

Denver's Indigent Defense System

A statewide public defender system has been part of the judicial branch in Colorado since the early 1970s. It is responsible for all indigent representation except in conflict cases. There are 18 regional trial offices with attorneys, two regional offices with only support staff (paralegals and investigators), and an appellate division. The system is administered by a state public defender, a chief trial deputy, a chief deputy, and an administrative unit of five (three professionals). The public defender is appointed by an independent public defender commission established by the supreme court.

The appointment of counsel in felony cases generally takes place in the Denver County Court. Colorado uses federal guidelines for determining indigency, but the information that defendants give is not verified. The public defender determines eligibility.

Colorado Public Defender in Denver

This office handles representation for the city and county of Denver. In 1987 the office had 27 staff attorneys and eight contract attorneys (only five of whom are state funded). There were 26 staff attorneys in 1990.

The Denver office is unique in several ways. First, many public defenders begin their employment doing misdemeanor and juvenile casework there and then move to other locations in the state. Denver proper is decreasing in caseload, so the office is not expanding. Because it is easy to find private attorneys to do contract work, contract attorneys are used in Denver for county court work on misdemeanors at the rate of $2,025 per month. A similar use of contract attorneys elsewhere in the state is not typical.

The majority of new attorneys come right out of law school. Individuals must be willing to go anywhere in the state. They must stay with an assignment 18 months before requesting a transfer to another office. In Denver, it will take two to two-and-a-half years to get a full felony caseload. Movement depends on the vacancy rate; with higher turnover, the move from entry to felony could take as little as 18 months. The attorneys handling juvenile cases will take some lesser adult felony cases before they move into the felony assignment.

Once every seven weeks, a felony attorney will be assigned to handle preliminary hearings and will thus pick up 15 to 30 new cases. Homicide cases are assigned statewide, in a separate rotation, to the most experienced attorneys. The individual prosecuting attorney receives the case about a week after it is filed. The office has open discovery, and case material is immediately made available to the defense counsel.

The average tenure of public defenders in Denver was six to seven years, with the statewide average estimated at five years. Salaries of public defenders statewide are higher than those of prosecuting attorneys; but in Denver, the salaries start off even, with the public defenders losing ground as they go up. Attorneys who leave tend to go into solo practice, although some have gone to private firms and judgeships.

The new hires begin with the county court misdemeanors, which in Denver means a contract position. Four-month contracts are extended for good lawyers until a staff vacancy occurs. Training is extensive, including weekly in-house training programs, mock pretrial presentations, a one-week "boot camp" patterned after the trial advocacy programs, and a yearly conference. The conference involves both in-house and outside presenters and qualifies for 15 continuing legal education credits. Private attorneys are invited to participate. Finally, speakers (e.g., a pathologist) make presentations about once a month.

Assigned Counsel

The court appoints counsel when the public defender must decline the representation of an indigent defendant. The assigned counsel attorneys indicate their areas of interest and expertise (e.g., misdemeanors, lesser felonies, more serious felonies), and appointments are taken from the appropriate lists. The judge determines the amount of reimbursement, but since 1985, the state public defender administers the funds appropriated. Control over the conflict budget by the state public defender has created an incentive to minimize conflicts and to scrutinize requests by assigned counsel for payments. The state public defender is said to earn credit with the state legislature by returning unspent funds at the end of the year.

Norfolk's Indigent Defense System

Representation of indigent defendants in the circuit court is provided by private attorneys who are appointed to individual cases. The lower (district) court generally makes appointments; however, the circuit court appoints counsel for indigent defendants when the cases do not originate in the lower court.

Appointment of counsel is made from a list of attorneys that is maintained by the circuit court but is also used by the district court. The list contains 78 names. There is apparently no formal process for getting on the list: an individual writes to the court and sets forth whatever information is deemed relevant (e.g., experience and references).

There were recent changes in how individuals received appointments. At one time, appointments were made from the list at the first appearance in the district court, with the attorney then being notified by mail that he or she had been appointed to a case. The approach had two shortcomings: First, the attorney was not present at the first appearance, thus missing an early opportunity to speak with the client. The attorney then had to arrange to see the client in jail or try to locate the individual in the community. Second, some attorneys contended that appointments were not being made equitably.

To address both issues, the district court now assigns attorneys to intake days. The designated attorney will be appointed to all new indigent cases that come before the court for first appearance on that day. With 78 people on the list, an attorney will have a "Duty Day" about once every two-and-a-half months. This system equalizes the number of appointments, or at least eliminates biased use of the list. A disadvantage, however, is that it treats the attorneys as fungible commodities and can result in inappropriate appointments when it is applied inflexibly by the court.

Compensation is by voucher. At the conclusion of the representation, the attorney completes a form indicating the total of in-court (compensated at the rate of $60 per hour) and out-of-court ($40 per hour) time.

The Virginia Bar has compulsory continuing legal education; other than that, there is no training requirement for appointed counsel. The assigned counsel attorneys who were interviewed had extensive experience and a varied civil and criminal practice. They acknowledged a wide range of experience and dedication among the members of the assigned counsel list, and distinguished better from worse lawyers by their diligence in attending the state bar criminal training programs and the extent to which they discussed strategy with other attorneys.

Monterey's Indigent Defense System

Monterey's indigent defense services are provided primarily by the Monterey County Public Defender's Office. Conflict cases are farmed out to a "consortium," which consists of six attorneys who contract with the county. Each consortium attorney handles a narrow range of cases and negotiates his own contract to provide those services. When neither the public defender's office nor a consortium attorney can be appointed, the court has a list of local attorneys on whom they can call.

Public Defender's Office

The public defender's office has a staff of 33 individuals: chief public defender, 2 assistant public defenders, 18 deputy public defenders, 7 secretaries, and 5 investigators. The office handles most of the indigent felony defendants. Felony cases are assigned to individual attorneys by the criminal division supervisor, taking work load and experience into account.

Most of the new attorneys have worked in another public defender's office, usually in a metropolitan area. There is a low turnover rate, and those who have left went on to be judges, defenders in other jurisdictions, and private attorneys. Training is primarily informal, by interoffice discussion, California Public Defender Association Briefs, bar courses, and communication with the bench.

Consortium

The county contracts with six attorneys to provide indigent representation in conflict cases. Each attorney submits a monthly claim with a list of her or his active caseload to receive a monthly check from the county. The attorneys must cover all of their expenses out of the contract (with the exception of investigative costs).

The consortium attorneys tend to be experienced criminal defense practitioners. All of them have been in practice for at least 15 years. They include attorneys with prior experience in the public defender's office, including one of the former heads of the office.

Assigned Counsel

When consortium attorneys are not able to take appointments, private attorneys are assigned. In 1987 there was no clear indication of what attorneys were eligible for these appointments, the process of how attorneys could be placed on the list was unspecified, and attorneys were not graded in a systematic way to handle different types of cases. More recently, the court has taken steps to formalize the assignment system by clarifying the criteria for appointment and what attorneys satisfy the criteria.

Globe's Indigent Defense System

Gila County contracts with private lawyers for indigent defense services. From 1986 through 1989, three lawyers held contracts. A fourth attorney was added to the contract system in 1990 to handle lesser felonies and juvenile dependency cases exclusively. Attorneys contract with the county board of supervisors, which funds indigent defense services. The system is not merely "low bid," however, and the court plays a meaningful role in awarding the contracts. Although the board of supervisors issues a request for proposals, bids are returned to the judges of the court. Thereafter, applicants negotiate their contracts with the court. The system for assigning cases to each of the contract attorneys blends work load and geographic considerations. In theory, each contract attorney receives an equal number of new cases each year. One of the indigent defense attorneys practices almost exclusively in a remote community within the county (Payson-Pine), and the other attorneys occasionally practice there.

All of the attorneys have a private practice in addition to the Gila County contract. One attorney estimates that 60 percent of his work was indigent defense and 40 percent private practice. Another attorney supplements his Gila County practice with additional contract indigent defense work in an adjacent county, which compensates him on a hourly rather than flat-fee basis. All of the attorneys maintain an office in Gila County, except for the recently hired contract attorney who handles the misdemeanors and less serious felony work.

In addition to selecting contract attorneys and regulating terms of contracts (in consultation with the supervisors), the judges also oversee the work load balance among attorneys. As a condition of receiving her or his monthly check, each attorney must submit a report each month showing the number of new cases, continuing cases, and closed cases. The trial court administrator processes the paperwork required for attorneys to get paid.

The judge determines eligibility based on a defendant's statements in open court. Appointments originate at the first appearance in the lower court for incarcerated defendants. Defendants who are released on bond or who are not in custody before the indictment are provided with counsel before arraignment in the upper court. Managing communications and procedure between the lower court and the upper court is sometimes problematic, according to the defense lawyers.

The three attorneys who handle felony cases are veteran lawyers with more than 15 years' experience in criminal practice, which includes 40 to 60 felony cases each year. In Globe, the superiority of experience by indigent defense counsel over the deputy prosecuting attorneys is apparent and generally acknowledged. They go to trial infrequently, but usually win when they do.

Oxford's Indigent Defense System

The state funds indigent defense in Maine, and Oxford County uses an assigned counsel system. A judge appoints attorneys from a list of available attorneys, with the assistance of the superior court clerk (in the instance of a direct indictment) and the chief deputy district court clerk (in the instance of a felony bindover). Attorneys who wish to be considered for assigned criminal cases inform the clerks of the respective courts who maintain the appointment lists. About 12 Oxford County lawyers accepted indigent criminal cases during the study period, with 6 of them receiving most of the appointments.

Although the state office manages the fiscal elements of the program, the local clerk of court processes the vouchers to get them approved by the judge and forwards them to the administrator in Portland. The state office reviews them and forwards them to Augusta for payment. Checks are written from the state capital in Augusta and mailed to the attorneys. Attorneys receive their checks four to ten weeks after submitting a voucher. The judges must approve vouchers submitted by counsel, and they may adjust the approved amount. The fee structure is set by the supreme court. No ceilings have been legislated for permissible attorney's fees, although the judge must approve the voucher. The judges have discretion to pay less than the full hourly rate.

Island's Indigent Defense System

Island delivers indigent defense services through an assigned counsel system. In the 1970s the Island County Defender's Association was formed to certify lawyers for the service, to manage referrals and appointments, and to negotiate with the board of commissioners over fee schedules. The association maintained a governing board and employed a secretary. The same secretary was hired later by the county commissioners as the full-time administrator of the indigent defense system. Through the association, the consortium of attorneys continued to speak to the county as a group, set standards for eligibility and, in effect, control admission to the indigent defense practice. Thus, even though Island is classified as an assigned system, it has important elements characteristic of a public defender system.

The indigent defense administrator for the Island County Defender's Association runs a tight ship with lots of statistics, careful scrutiny of appointment documentation and the fees charged, review of defendant eligibility, and determination of partial ability to pay. She is responsible for controlling the quality of services, handling fiscal matters, and getting promissory notes when clients have some ability to pay. There is an expectation that attorneys will meet with clients within 48 hours of admission to jail.

All defendants who wish assigned counsel are interviewed and must complete an eligibility determination form. Some are screened out as ineligible and are advised about ways to borrow money. If they are deemed ineligible, defendants either secure their own lawyer or, if they show evidence of unsuccessful attempts to secure loans, they may be reevaluated for appointed counsel. In these cases, there will be a promissory note and judgment to pay all or part of the fees on a payment schedule.

The assigned counsel system matches attorneys to case severity, with the more experienced attorneys getting the more serious cases. There are approximately 12 attorneys on the assigned counsel roster, all of whom have had several years of experience. Judges and other court personnel state that Island County's system appears to represent the values that should be present in a system of criminal defense—access to experienced attorneys who specialize in trial practice and criminal law and the opportunity for a "personal" relationship.

San Juan's Indigent Defense System

San Juan is an island community with no bridges to the mainland. Indigent defense service has been provided there since 1980 through a contract system. Before that time, defense was provided by an assigned counsel system, similar to Oxford County's. Most attorneys accepted appointments reluctantly, however. From 1979 to 1980, some local lawyers lobbied the county to increase the fee schedule; instead, a contract system was initiated by the county commissioners. Until recently, the contract was strictly on a low-bid criterion. The contract attorney assumed responsibility for all criminal, juvenile, and mental health cases, including all overhead. The court at the time was passive, under the theory that so long as there was a vehicle for appointment of counsel, the commissioners were free to fund the service in whatever manner they saw fit.

During the first year of the contract program, the contract attorney moved from the island to a mainland community, three hours distant by automobile and ferry. Thereafter, until 1990, a succession of three attorneys who did not live in the county held the contracts. One of these attorneys had previously been the deputy prosecutor responsible for criminal cases. Throughout this period there was general dissatisfaction with the contract service among the bar and criminal justice community, but there were no organized attempts to intervene with the commissioners. Complaints generally had to do with the unavailability of the lawyer at critical times. Not only was the lawyer rarely available to clients immediately following arrest, but he often would be late for, or entirely miss, scheduled court appearances. These proceedings would have to be rescheduled.

On the retirement of the senior judge in 1989, the judges opened discussion with the county commissioners about adopting standards for indigent defense (following a statewide trend in Washington). Most significant for San Juan County was the mutual agreement by the county commissioners and the court that indigent defense must be provided by a resident attorney.

There was virtually no management of the program during the study period. Once the contract was let, neither the court nor the executive branch maintained any program controls. There were no caseload or work load data, no statements of service, and no criteria for eligibility or competence. The lawyers who did get the contract, however, were all very experienced criminal lawyers who had practiced criminal law in public defender's offices, prosecuting attorney's offices, and the judge advocate general's office.

Context of Indigent Defense: Comparative Overview

The similarities and differences among the nine courts are highlighted below along three basic dimensions: (1) their environment, (2) their organization, and (3) the prosecutor's office. Where does each court stand in terms of the size of the population that it serves; the percent of all felony dispositions handled by appointed attorneys rather than privately retained attorneys; and the type of organization, management, and experience of deputy prosecutors?

Environment

As seen in **Table 3**, the communities served by the nine courts have distinctive social and economic characteristics.[24] (Because the case-related data are based on felony dispositions in 1987, the communities' characteristics are measured in terms of the most current data on the counties served by the courts as of 1987 compiled by the U.S. Bureau of the Census). On every dimension ranging from population size to the rate of violent crimes, there is a wide range. The communities extend in size from over two million (Detroit) to less than ten thousand (San Juan). Denver has a violent

---

[24] All of the courts, except the Norfolk Circuit Court, have jurisdictional boundaries that are coterminous with a single county. The Norfolk court serves the city of Norfolk. The only other slightly unusual jurisdictional feature arises in Denver District Court, where the city and county of Denver are one and the same.

Table 3
What Do the Communities Look Like?

	Detroit	Seattle	Denver	Norfolk	Monterey	Globe	Oxford	Island	San Juan
1986 Population	2,154,300	1,362,300	505,000	274,800	339,700	39,700	50,200	49,600	9,200
Percent Change in Population, 1980-86	-7.4	7.3	2.5	2.9	17.0	7.1	2.4	12.6	17.3
Median Household Income, 1979	18,629	20,717	15,506	12,509	17,658	13,238	13,029	15,600	16,026
Percent Under Poverty Level, 1979	14.3	7.7	13.7	20.7	11.4	16.2	12.7	9.9	12.0
Percent of Population that Is Black and Other, 1984	38.9	8.5	16.0	38.4	15.4	14.2	.5	6.4	—
Per Capita Income, 1985	10,681	13,192	12,490	9,340	10,420	7,399	8,379	10,058	12,337
Percent of Female Head of Household, 1980	16.9	8.5	10.4	16.4	9.5	8.3	8.5	6.3	6.0
Violent Crime Per 100,000 Population, 1985	9,864	8,463	10,557	6,561	5,419	2,476	1,781	2,278	2,483

crime rate of 10,557 per 100,000 population, and at the other end of the spectrum, Oxford has a rate of 1,781 per 100,000.

The profiles of the individual communities defy the classification schemes that other researchers have used to categorize communities in their studies.[25] As an illustration, Denver and Monterey are similar in terms of median household income, the proportion of the population living in poverty, and the proportion of the population that is black or of another nonwhite race. On the other hand, Denver has a crime rate that is twice as large and a population growth that is seven times smaller than Monterey's respective rates. The greatest similarity exists between the two small-sized, adjacent communities in Washington State. Island and San Juan Counties look alike on most dimensions, although Island has 49,600 residents and San Juan has 9,200 residents. Finally, there is some clustering among the four small-sized courts (Globe, Oxford, Island, and San Juan). These courts look alike on the dimensions of crime, income, and the proportion of female head of households. However, these four small courts stand apart from each other on other key factors, such as racial composition and population change. Hence, it seems fair and accurate to infer that the nine courts operate within diverse environments.

What Do the Courts Look Like?

All the courts are part of a two-tiered judicial system, one of the few consistencies to be found in the courts' organizational structures. For example, the assumption that in two-tiered systems, individuals charged with felony offenses have their first appearances and preliminary hearings in one court and are bound over to the other court for arraignment and trial holds true for only some of the nine courts. The exceptions are Norfolk and Oxford, where the grand jury is used extensively. The other exceptions are Seattle, Island, and San Juan, where felony charges generally are filed directly in the superior court (see **Table 4**).

The courts also vary according to their basic calendaring practices, with five courts using individual calendars, two using master calendars, and two using hybrids. The greatest uniformity exists in areas, such as the lack of plea routing (plea routing means that the judges who sentence defendants who plead guilty are different from the judges who sentence those defendants who are convicted in a trial) in all courts (except Detroit) and continuous terms for judges in all courts (except Oxford and San Juan).[26] Yet, although the courts are organized differently, they are confronted with similar work.

---

[25] For example, Nardulli, Eisenstein, and Flemming put the nine courts that they studied into three categories called ring, autonomous, and declining counties. Ring counties are prosperous, suburban counties with fairly homogenous populations (e.g., Oakland, Michigan). Declining counties have populations with low to moderate incomes, social cleavages, and a declining industrial base (e.g., Saginaw, Michigan). Autonomous counties are economically between the extremes of ring and declining counties but have less politically insulated courts than do ring counties (e.g., Kalamazoo, Michigan).

[26] In San Juan County there is one weekly law and motion day, but trial "terms" are scheduled on an as-needed basis, since the judges "ride circuit" to San Juan County from their county of residence.

Table 4
Felony Courts—Structure, Calendaring, and Scheduling Practices

	Detroit	Seattle	Denver	Norfolk	Monterey	Globe	Oxford	San Juan and Island
Type of Docket	Specialized	Specialized (rotating)	Specialized (rotating)	Mixed (rotating)	Mixed	Mixed	Mixed	Mixed
Number of Judges	54	45	20	9	8	2	1	2
Number of Judges Hearing Criminal Cases	34	15	6	4-5	4	All	All	All
Type of Term	Continuous	Continuous	Continuous	Continuous	Continuous	Continuous	Periodic	Continuous
Type of Calendar	Hybrid (team)	Hybrid (team)	Individual	Master	Master	Individual	Individual	Individual
Method of Assigning Cases to Judge	Blind	Random After Omnibus	Personalized (Pre-set Arraignment Days)	Blind	Blind	Random	Not Applicable	
Availability of Plea Routing	Yes	No	No	No	No	No	No	No
Route to Felony Court	Lower Court Bindovers Without Grand Jury. Direct Indictment Rare.	Most Felonies Directly Filed. Direct Indictment Rare.	Lower Court Bindovers Through Grand Jury. Direct Indictment Rare.	Lower Court Bindovers Through Grand Jury. Direct Indictment from Grand Jury.	Lower Court Bindovers Without Grand Jury. Direct Indictment Rare.	Lower Court Bindovers Without Grand Jury. Some Direct Indictments.	Lower Court Bindovers Through Grand Jury. Direct Indictment.	Direct File of Most Felonies. Direct Indictment Rare.

Table 5
Caseload Composition in the Courts
Felony Dispositions, 1987

Most Serious Offense Charged	Detroit	Seattle	Denver	Norfolk	Monterey	Globe	Oxford	Island	San Juan
Crimes Against the Person	22.1% (101)	23.6% (143)	33.5% (124)	21.6% (100)	18.1% (74)	21.8% (37)	36.3% (81)	18.4% (23)	12.9 % (4)
Burglary/Theft	33.5% (153)	44.7% (271)	40.8% (151)	50.1% (232)	40.2% (164)	28.2% (48)	28.7% (64)	48.0% (60)	45.2 % (14)
Drug Sale and Possession	19.2% (88)	17.8% (108)	19.2% (71)	17.7% (82)	32.6% (133)	24.1% (41)	5.8% (13)	24.8% (31)	35.5 % (11)
Other Felonies	25.2% (115)	13.9% (84)	6.5% (24)	10.6% (49)	9.1% (37)	25.9% (44)	29.1% (65)	8.8% (11)	6.5% (2)
Totals	100% (457)	100% (606)	100% (370)	100% (463)	100% (408)	100% (170)	100% (223)	100% (125)	100% (31)

The caseload composition of the courts is strikingly similar in several respects (see **Table 5**). First, burglary and theft account for the largest proportion of offenses charged against defendants in all courts except Oxford.[27] In Oxford, crimes against the person and other types of felonies are more frequent than burglary and theft. Second, the relative frequency of crimes against the person (e.g., homicide, robbery, kidnapping, sexual abuse) is similar for seven of the nine courts. Oxford and San Juan, which have the largest and smallest proportions of crimes against the person, are polar opposites that stand apart from the other courts. Third, the volume of drug sale and possession cases is less than either crimes against the person or burglary and theft charges in most of the courts. Hence, the relative size of each offense category, but not necessarily the specific proportions, are reasonably consistent across all courts.

What Do the Prosecutors' Offices Look Like?

The prosecutors' offices are as varied as court organization (see **Table 6**). There is no uniform case assignment system. Horizontal representation occurs as frequently as vertical representation. Plea authority is generally in the hands of individual attorneys, but a centralized approach is also found in large (Detroit), midsized (Monterey) and small (Island) offices.[28] Even the expectation that the

---

[27] Offenses are classified according to the most serious felony offense, although information on all offenses was collected.

[28] In Island County the elected prosecutor during the study years exercised very close supervision over screening, filing, and plea decisions, i.e. the functional equivalent of specialized screening and centralized plea authority.

Table 6
Prosecution Screening, Plea Authority, and Staffing Structure

	Detroit	Seattle	Denver	Norfolk	Monterey	Globe	Oxford	San Juan and Island
Does Prosecutor Screen?	Yes	Yes	Yes	No	Yes	Yes	Yes	Yes
Type of Screening	Separate Unit of Experienced Staff	Separate Unit, Not Necessarily Experienced	Experienced Attorneys Rotate into Screening	Not Applicable	Separate Screening Attorney	Attorney Assigned to the Case	Usually an Attorney; Sometimes a Paralegal	I: By Elected Prosecutor. SJ: By Deputy Prosecutors
Plea Authority	Centralized	Initial Offer Set by Filing Attorney; Centralized Pre-omnibus	Authority in Individual Attorney	Authority in Individual Attorney	Centralized	Authority in Individual Attorney	Authority in Individual Attorney	I: Approved by Elected Prosecutor SJ: Authority in Individual Attorney
Staffing	Horizontal	Horizontal	Vertical from Preliminary Hearing	Vertical from Preliminary Hearing	Vertical from Preliminary Hearing	Vertical	Horizontal	Vertical
Number of Attorneys (Year)	152 (1989)	120 (1987)	48 (1989)	18 (1989)	26 (1988)	4 (1989)	1 (1989)	I: 5 SJ: 2 (1989)
Average Attorney Tenure	3-6 Years	2-4 Years	4-7 Years	4-7 Years	5-8 Years	2-4 Years	5-7 Years	I: 4-6 Years SJ: 3-5 Years

prosecutor will screen cases is not consistent for all the courts. In Norfolk, there is no screening.

Most of the prosecutors' offices hire individuals with limited experience, as is the case with most of the public defenders' offices. In most of the communities, deputies are hired after they graduate and pass the bar. In all of the communities (including Seattle, where attorneys may be hired before graduating and passing the bar), new attorneys may have some experience ranging from an internship, clerkship, judge advocates general, or previous private practice. In all of the communities, moreover, an attorney fresh from law school begins by working on misdemeanor and routine juvenile cases.

The retention of attorneys and the accumulation of experience may be more salient issues than that of initial recruitment. The issues are framed in terms of whether new attorneys stay beyond the first one or two years, and what the typical tenure is thereafter. In large and small communities alike, deputy prosecutors typically remain for three to five years. Small communities do not appear to differ from the large communities in this regard. In the small communities, keeping new deputies on the job for more than one or two years was a problem for some (Globe and Island County) but not for others (Oxford and San Juan counties.) The professional and social opportunities in nearby metropolitan areas, including the possibility of working in larger prosecutors' offices, the U.S. Attorney's Office, and private practice, were given as the reasons for the former, while the lure of a nonurban setting was given as a reason for the latter. Consequently, the problem of retention is not uniform across all of the small courts.

Assistant prosecutors remaining in the office for ten or more years is an upper limit and achieved only occasionally. To the extent that the estimates of the managing prosecutors are accurate, the prosecutors' offices in these nine courts are not in a superior position compared to indigent defenders in procuring experienced trial counsel. None of the evidence from the interviews with deputy prosecutors and indigent defense attorneys, in fact, showed that the prosecutor's office is in a position to overwhelm indigent defenders.

Finally, the nature of training available to prosecutors varies among the courts.[29] Predictably, in the small communities, training for prosecutors is limited to programs offered out-of-county by the state prosecutor's association or the bar. In the larger communities, some prosecutors' offices offer in-house training (Denver and Seattle), and some do not (Detroit and Norfolk). Where there is training, in-house seminars supplement one-week programs for new prosecutors offered by the state

---

[29] There is one exception: all of the offices that hire some deputies straight from initially passing the bar use assignment to misdemeanor practice as the linchpin of an on-the-job training program.

prosecutor's association. Other methods, such as extensive manuals and procedures (Seattle) and annual retreats (Denver), provide the entire office with the opportunity to discuss new laws and policies.

It is not possible to judge whether the training afforded prosecuting attorneys is superior to that received by indigent defenders. The training opportunities afforded indigent defenders, however, are as ample as those of prosecuting attorneys. Hence, prosecutors enjoy no special advantage over indigent defenders when it comes to training.[30]

Summary

Indigent defense should be thought of as a flexible system of interrelated elements rather than three mutually exclusive structures. There is no doubt that there are public defenders, assigned counsel, and contract attorneys and that the methods by which they receive appointments tend to be different. Looking at these systems in the nine courts, however, the following three lessons emerge:

(1) There is no single organizational model of public defenders, assigned counsel, or contract attorneys. There are important variants within each of these three categories.

(2) Virtually all possible combinations of public defenders, assigned counsel, and contract attorneys are feasible. Courts can design the arrangements that meet their particular needs and circumstances.

(3) Indigent defense systems should not be assessed simply in terms of organizational structure and the assumed advantages of the preferred structure. Instead, the performance of a given structure should be measured in terms of how well the indigent defenders actually handle their cases. That topic is the subject of the next two chapters.

---

[30] An apparent advantage prosecutors may have over indigent defenders is the existence in many states of a prosecuting attorneys' association with a paid staff. This may provide opportunities for the prosecutor to receive specialized training that is not available to the defense practitioner in the smaller community. But in the larger counties where there is a public defender office, in-house training programs provided to the public defenders match the offerings of the state prosecutor associations.

Chapter III
Timeliness

Timeliness

Introduction

The expeditious resolution of criminal cases is both a right guaranteed under the U.S. Constitution and a standard to which courts are held accountable. According to the sixth amendment, defendants are entitled to a speedy trial as well as the assistance of counsel. Consequently, indigent defenders have a fiduciary obligation to avoid unnecessary delays.

Timeliness is also a goal that the courts are expected to achieve. Both the American Bar Association (ABA) and the Conference of State Court Administrators (COSCA) have stipulated standards for courts. Specifically, the ABA states that all felony cases should take no longer than one year from the date of the arrest to be adjudicated. It is expected, moreover, that most cases should take considerably less than one year to reach final disposition. According to the ABA, 90 percent of all felony cases should be adjudicated within 120 days from the date of arrest, and 98 percent should be adjudicated within 180 days from the date of arrest.[31]

This chapter addresses three questions. How much time do indigent defenders and privately retained attorneys typically take to resolve felony cases? Do different types of attorneys take longer (or shorter) lengths of time to dispose of their cases? Are indigent defenders quicker (or slower) than privately retained attorneys after taking the various types of offense and types of disposition into account?

These questions are addressed in three ways. First, information is presented on the typical length of time that indigent defenders and privately retained attorneys take to resolve felony cases in each of the nine courts. The span of time is measured in both the elapsed number of days from the date of arrest to adjudication and the elapsed number of days from the date of the indictment/information to adjudication.[32] These two time periods are used because of the unreliability of arrest dates in some cases and because in some courts the use of grand jury proceedings means that the starting point of the process is the date of indictment. The typical length of

---

[31] *See* American Bar Association, Standards Relating to Trial Courts as Amended secs. 2.50 - 2.52 (1987).

[32] Adjudication is the entry of a dismissal, guilty plea, deferred adjudication, diversion, or verdict.

processing time is measured in the median number of days. The median number of days (e.g., 100) means that half of the cases handled by a particular type of attorney (e.g., public defender) took less than 100 days to be adjudicated and that half the cases took more than 100 days to be adjudicated.

Second, the proportion of cases that take over 180 days to be resolved is estimated for each type of attorney in every court. According to the ABA Standards, this figure should not exceed 2 percent.

Third, attorneys from each court are combined with the same type of attorneys in the other courts (e.g., public defenders in Seattle, Detroit, Denver, and Monterey are grouped together) in order to have a sufficient number of cases on which to conduct statistical tests. The question is then asked, do the different groups of attorneys (e.g., public defenders versus privately retained counsel) take distinctively different amounts of time to dispose of their cases after taking the various types of offense and types of disposition into account? The technique of the analysis of variance is used to gauge whether the differences, if any, are statistically significant.

Length of Time from Arrest to Disposition

The indigent defenders consistently process the typical case in less time than privately retained attorneys, except in Island County. The median number of days from the date of arrest to the date of adjudication for indigent defenders is less than it is for privately retained counsel in each of the eight other courts for all types of indigent defenders except for the small group of assigned counsel in Monterey (see **Table 7**). In Monterey, the median number of days to adjudication for assigned counsel (115) is longer than the median for privately retained counsel (89 days). However, both the public defenders (56 days) and the contract attorneys (78 days), which are the primary and secondary providers of indigent defense in Monterey, are faster than privately retained counsel (89 days).

Meeting the ABA Standard

The same pattern of positive performance by indigent defenders emerges when the ABA Standard of resolving 98 percent of felony cases within 180 days of the arrest date is used. Interestingly, only San Juan meets the standard; in the other eight courts, more than 2 percent of the felony cases are still open at 180 days. However, the percent of cases remaining open after 180 days is consistently less for the indigent defenders in all the courts except Globe (see **Table 8**). In Globe, 28.6 percent of the cases represented by contract attorneys remain open after 180 days, and 27.2 percent of the cases represented by private attorneys remain open after 180 days from the date of arrest. Additionally, in Monterey, relatively more of the cases with privately

Table 7
What Is the Typical Length of Time that Indigent Defenders and Privately Retained Counsel Take to Resolve Cases?
Median Number of Days from the Date of Arrest to Adjudication*

	Detroit	Seattle**	Denver	Norfolk	Monterey	Globe	Oxford	Island	San Juan
Public Defender	79	75	151	–	56	–	–	–	–
Contract Attorney	–		–	–	78	125	–	–	79
Assigned Counsel	62	–	162	114	115	–	134	156	–
Privately Retained Counsel	102	101	167	184	89	141	215	131	88
All Cases	71	85	156	126	63	129	161	146	83

* Adjudication is the entry of a dismissal, guilty plea, deferred adjudication, diversion, or verdict.

** In Seattle, the indigent defense attorneys represented are from three public defender firms: The Defender Association (TDA); Associated Counsel for the Accused (ACA); Society of Counsel Representing Accused Persons (SCRAP). The typical case-processing time for each firm is as follows: TDA (89 days); ACA (77 days), and SCRAP (59 days).

Table 8
Do Indigent Defenders or Privately Retained Counsel More Closely Approximate the ABA's Time Standards?
Percent of Felony Cases Unresolved After 180 Days from the Arrest
ABA Standards Stipulate that 2 Percent or Less of the Cases Should Be Unresolved

	Detroit	Seattle**	Denver	Norfolk	Monterey	Globe	Oxford	Island	San Juan
Public Defender	16.7%	19.0%	43.8%	–	8.3%	–	–	–	–
Contract Attorney	–		–	–	3.9%	28.6%	–	–	0%
Assigned Counsel	11.9%		45.5%	20.9%	20.0%	–	42.4%	44.6%	–
Privately Retained Attorneys	21.8%	26.4%	45.6%	51.1%	11.5%	27.2%	60.0%	47.2%	9.1%
All Cases	14.4%	21.1%	44.2%	29.7%	8.0%	28.3%	49.1%	45.6%	3.4%

* In Seattle, the indigent defense attorneys represented are from three public defender firms: The Defender Association (TDA); Associated Counsel for the Accused (ACA); Society of Counsel Representing Accused Persons (SCRAP). The percentages of unresolved cases after 180 days for the three firms are as follows: TDA (23.0%); ACA (17.6%); and SCRAP (16.3%).

retained counsel meet the ABA Standard than do the cases with assigned counsel. However, the two larger groups of indigent defenders in Monterey (public defender and contract attorneys) approximate the standard more closely than do the privately retained attorneys.

Upper-court-processing Time

An examination of the length of time from indictment/information to disposition puts all of the courts on more or less equal footing. The time taken to resolve cases in the upper court screens out the possible effects of the different paths taken to get to the indictment stage (e.g., bindover from a lower court, direct filing, grand jury). However, there is no particular ABA Standard that governs this segment of the process. Hence, the speed of upper-court case-processing time is measured by using the median number of days that each type of defense attorney takes to resolve its set of cases.

Cases involving indigent defenders move faster than cases involving privately retained counsel in almost all of the courts (see **Table 9**). In Denver and Island, privately retained attorneys are more expeditious, on average, than their counterparts in the indigent defense community. In Monterey, the privately retained cases take less time than those represented by assigned counsel, but they are not as expeditious as public defenders and contract attorneys. Finally, in Globe, the median case-processing times for the contract attorneys and the privately retained attorneys are dead even at 102 days.

In summary, the indigent defenders look good viewed through the lenses of timeliness and the ABA Standards, in particular. They are performing as well as privately retained counsel in almost all of the courts in terms of the length of time from arrest to disposition, upper-court case-processing time, and the ABA Standard of resolving 98 percent of the cases within 180 days from the date of arrest. However, it is not obvious that the observable differences in case-processing times are attributable to the different types of attorneys. For example, do indigent defenders generally conclude their cases more quickly because their cases involve less-serious offenses? Do they process cases more quickly because more of their cases involve guilty pleas, which generally take less time to reach trial than adjudications?

The Effects of Defense Counsel on Case-processing Time

This section sorts out the effects of the type of attorney from other factors, such as the various types of offense and the various methods of disposition. Are there statistically significant differences in case-processing times even after taking the different types of offenses into account? Are some types of attorneys more expeditious in handling cases that go to trial as well as those that are disposed of short of trial? If these questions are answered affirmatively, then they indicate that the type of attorney makes a difference in the pace of litigation. If these questions are answered negatively, then they indicate that whether a case moves quickly or slowly through the legal process has little to do with the type of attorney handling the case.

Chapter III Timeliness

Table 9
Is the Upper-court Case-processing Time for Indigent Defenders Shorter or Longer than for Privately Retained Counsel?
Median Number of Days from the Date of Indictment/Information to Adjudication
Felony Dispositions

	Detroit	Seattle**	Denver	Norfolk	Monterey	Globe	Oxford	Island	San Juan
Public Defender	67	68	111	-	15	-	-	-	-
Contract Attorney	-	-	-	-	30	102	-	-	77
Assigned Counsel	45	-	129	58	45	-	175	50	-
Privately Retained Attorneys	86	96	102	98	36	102	196	45	84
All Cases	54	73	111	69	23	102	176	49	82

* In Seattle, the indigent defense attorneys represented are from three public defender firms: The Defender Association (TDA); Associated Counsel for the Accused (ACA); Society of Counsel Representing Accused Persons (SCRAP). The typical case-processing time for each firm is as follows: TDA (80 days), ACA (61 days), and SCRAP (63 days).

Table 10
Is the Type of Criminal Defense Attorney Associated with the Pace of Litigation?
Felony Dispositions from Nine General Jurisdiction Trial Courts

Average Number of Days from Date of Indictment/Information to Adjudication

Public Defenders	Contract Attorneys	Assigned Counsel	Privately Retained Attorney
128 days	115 days	103 days	160 days
(n = 1183)	(n = 213)	(n = 866)	(n = 590)

F=6.346   Significance Level=.001

These questions are addressed by combining each type of defense attorney from the nine different courts into four separate groups (i.e., public defender, contract attorney, assigned counsel, and privately retained counsel) in order to have a sufficient number of cases on which to conduct statistical tests. The empirical question is, are the groups closely knit or are they distinct from one another in the time that it takes them to resolve cases? If they are distinctively different, what groups are slower (or faster) than others and under what conditions?

There are statistically significant differences in the average (arithmetic mean) case-processing times among the various types of defense attorneys (see **Table 10**).

Privately retained counsel take 160 days, on average, to resolve their cases in the upper court, whereas public defenders (128 days), contract attorneys (115 days), and assigned counsel (103 days) are increasingly more expeditious. The results are significant at the .001 level, which means that the observed pattern could have happened by chance alone only one time out of a thousand. The type of criminal defense attorney makes a substantial difference in the extent to which cases are resolved in a timely manner, and all three types of indigent defenders are significantly more timely than privately retained attorneys.[33] However, this important finding is limited because the effects of other factors on case-processing time are not screened out. An effort must be made to siphon off the effects of rival explanations for the speedier case processing by indigent defenders (e.g., they handle less-serious cases, which are by themselves more likely to be resolved quickly).

The results in Table 10 are explored in greater depth in three ways. First, are there similar differences between privately retained counsel and indigent defenders in both cases that go to trial and cases that do not? It is important to account for this factor because retained attorneys go to trial relatively more frequently than do indigent defenders.[34] Second, are there differences among the types of attorneys when the type of offense is taken into account? This factor is important because indigent defenders may handle slightly more of the most serious offenses than privately retained attorneys. Third, do the different types of attorneys have different case-processing times when both the various methods of disposition and the various types of offenses are taken into account?

---

[33] The method for analyzing the data involves the application of the analysis-of-variance statistical technique. The raw data consist of the elapsed number of days from the date of the indictment to the date of the final disposition for each case. Upper-court time is used because arrest dates are not available or are unreliable in many instances.

The analysis of variance indicates whether the average (arithmetic mean) case-processing times for each of the four groups of criminal defense attorneys are significantly different. The technique determines whether the variation in case-processing times among each of the groups is greater (or lesser) than the variation between each group. Each group must be fairly homogenous (like a neighborhood) rather than heterogeneous (like a conglomerate) in order for the technique to indicate that the groups are associated with significantly different average case-processing times.

The technique produces an F-statistic that measures the ratio of intergroup to intragroup variation. A positive F-statistic means that the variation between the four groups of attorneys is greater than the variation within each group. That is, the four groups of attorneys have different case-processing times. A test of significance applied to the F-statistic indicates whether the observed results could have happened by chance alone (e.g., a .01 significance level means that the results could have happened by chance alone 1 out of 100 times, and .0001 means that the results could happen by chance alone 1 out of 10,000 times). Hence, the smaller the significance level, the greater the confidence that can be placed in the inference that different types of attorneys are linked to distinctive case-processing times. For this inquiry, the conventional benchmark of .05 is used. That means that the significance level must be .05 or smaller in order to conclude that groups of defense attorneys have significantly different case-processing times.

[34] The trial rates for the four categories of defense attorneys are similar. Privately retained counsel have a higher rate, however, than the indigent defenders. The rates for the various categories of attorneys are as follows: public defenders (10 percent), contract attorneys (7 percent), assigned counsel (10 percent), and privately retained counsel (14 percent).

Table 11
Is the Type of Criminal Defense Attorney Associated with the Pace of Litigation Controlling for the Type of Disposition?
Felony Dispositions from Nine General Jurisdiction Courts

Public Defenders		Contract Attorneys		Assigned Counsel		Privately Retained Attorney	
Trials	Nontrials	Trials	Nontrials	Trials	Nontrials	Trials	Nontrials
160 days	124 days	122 days	114 days	137 days	99 days	194 days	155 days
(n=118)	(n=1,065)	(n=4)	(n=199)	(n=102)	(n=764)	(n=82)	(n=508)

F=3.601   Significance Level=.001

Table 12
Is the Type of Criminal Defense Attorney Associated with the Pace of Litigation Controlling for the Type of Offense?
Felony Dispositions from Nine General Jurisdiction Courts

Average Number of Days from the Date of Indictment/Information to Adjudication

	Public Defenders	Contract Attorneys	Assigned Counsel	Privately Retained Counsel
Crimes Against the Person	139 (274)	226 (37)	144 (199)	173 (177)
Drug Sale/ Possession	99 (238)	117 (56)	90 (125)	166 (159)
Burglary/Theft	134 (527)	72 (76)	94 (397)	149 (156)
Other Types of Felonies	134 (144)	95 (44)	88 (145)	146 (98)

F=2.777   Significance Level=.001

The empirical answers to these questions are displayed in Tables 11, 12, and 13. The initial evidence, presented in Table 10, that indigent defenders are more timely holds up. All three tables indicate that the differences between the groups of attorneys are statistically significant. Substantively, privately retained attorneys take longer when they go to trial (194 days, on average) than do public defenders (160 days), assigned counsel (137 days), or contract attorneys (122 days) (see **Table 11**). And they also take longer to achieve nontrial dispositions (155 days, on average) than do public defenders (124 days), assigned counsel (99 days), or contract attorneys (115 days). Hence, when the mode of disposition is taken into account, indigent defenders perform better. The same pattern appears in **Table 12**. Privately retained attorneys consistently have longer case-processing times for each of the general offense

Table 13
Does the Type of Criminal Defense Attorney Make a Difference in the Pace of Litigation Controlling for the Type of Disposition and the Type of Offense? Felony Dispositions from Nine General Jurisdiction Courts

Average Number of Days from the Date of Indictment/Information to Adjudication

	Public Defenders		Assigned Counsel		Privately Retained Counsel	
	Trials	Nontrials	Trials	Nontrials	Trials	Nontrials
Crimes Against the Person	161 (58)	132 (216)	147 (58)	142 (141)	207 (33)	166 (144)
Drug Sale/ Possession	217 (19)	89 (219)	152 (14)	82 (111)	163 (18)	167 (141)
Burglary and Theft	132 (27)	134 (500)	100 (17)	93 (380)	194 (14)	144 (142)
Other Types of Felonies	130 (14)	134 (130)	125 (13)	84 (132)	202 (17)	134 (81)

F=1.685   Significance Level=.022

categories. The only exception occurs in crimes against the person where contract attorneys take 226 days, on average, and privately retained attorneys take 173 days, on average, to resolve cases involving these types of offenses.

Public defenders and assigned counsel are more expeditious than privately retained counsel even when controlling simultaneously for the method of disposition and the type of offense.[35] The pace of litigation is significantly different among the three groups of attorneys (see **Table 13**). Assigned counsel are the most expeditious, followed by public defenders, which means that both groups resolve their cases more quickly than privately retained counsel. Retained counsel take, on average, more time to resolve their cases, whether by trial or nontrial and whether the case involves crimes against the person or some other offense. There are some exceptions to this pattern. Trial dispositions in drug sale/possession cases take longer for public defenders to resolve (217 days) than for privately retained counsel (163 days). And there are situations in which public defenders are more expeditious than assigned counsel. As an illustration, nontrial dispositions of crimes against the person are handled, on average, in 132 days by public defenders and 142 days, on

---

[35] Because of the limited number of contract attorneys, they cannot be included in the analysis. There are too few of them in some of the combinations of disposition types and offense types to permit a valid statistical test.

average, by assigned counsel. However, the overall pattern to the data is one in which assigned counsel are the most expeditious and privately retained counsel the least expeditious.

Summary

The importance of timeliness is rooted in the basic American commitment to efficiency. There are few individuals in this society who argue for inefficiency.[36] It is not surprising that the American Bar Association has promulgated time standards that its members and that the courts should strive to meet. Moreover, timeliness is not seen as incompatible with other core values surrounding the basic notion of justice. Recently, a national commission of trial court judges and court administrators incorporated timeliness into a larger set of values that includes access to justice; equality, fairness, and integrity; independence and accountability; and public trust and confidence.[37] Hence, it seems reasonable to expect indigent defenders to resolve their cases expeditiously and to compare their performance with that of privately retained counsel.

The quantitative results, which indicate that indigent defenders do well in terms of timeliness, have profound implications. One implication is that the expeditious adjudication of cases reduces the demand for additional court appearances and the length of time that defendants spend in jail awaiting disposition of their cases. Assembling all the participants in the legal process for court proceedings and the pretrial detaining of defendants are undeniably costly. Hence, indigent defenders contribute to cost savings by their timeliness.

Second, the closer approximation by indigent defenders to established time standards presents a picture that diverges from the popular image. A common view of indigent defenders is that they are engaging in dilatory tactics in one case in order to meet deadlines in other cases. Simply stated, they are viewed as unable to schedule their work, to satisfy time requirements, and to live within budgetary constraints. That point of view is not supported by the data from the nine courts under study. In terms of approximating time standards, indigent defenders perform better than privately retained attorneys. What other public institutions can make the claim that they perform as well as the private sector?

---

[36] However, there are individuals, including well-known judges, who contend that delay benefits the justice system. *See* Bazelon, *New Gods for Old*, 46 New York University Law Review 653 (1971).

[37] Commission on Trial Court Performance Standards, *Trial Court Performance Standards with Commentary* (National Center for State Courts 1990).

Third, the achievement of timeliness frames the issue of effective representation in a new light. Instead of engaging in a philosophical debate over whether timeliness is inherently good or bad, one can ask the empirical question, are the gains in efficiency made at the expense of the defendants? Are the rights or interests of defendants sacrificed in some way? The achievement of timeliness needs to be viewed side by side with information on the outcomes for defendants. The tasks of presenting and interpreting the needed information are the subject of the next chapter.

Chapter IV
Performance and Indigent Defense

Performance and Indigent Defense

Introduction

There are two basic approaches to assessing the performance of indigent defenders in the literature. The first approach has what may be called an input orientation. Indigent defenders are expected to represent their clients by being adequately prepared—meeting with clients, contacting witnesses, conducting research, and carefully reviewing presentence investigation reports and so forth. Hence, a body of guidelines has been formulated that identifies how effective representation is to be conducted.[38]

The second approach has what may be called an output orientation. Indigent defenders are expected to represent their clients by achieving favorable outcomes, such as acquittals and dismissals, charge reductions, noncustodial sentences, and the shortest possible periods of incarceration. Using this approach, the extent to which indigent defenders are performing successfully is determined by comparing them to privately retained counsel and by asking whether indigent defenders achieve the same proportion of favorable outcomes for their clients as privately retained counsel achieve for theirs.[39] This comparison sets a high standard of evaluation for indigent defenders. There are several factors that have very little to do with the relative capabilities of attorneys that make it more difficult for indigent than nonindigent defendants to gain favorable outcomes. First, indigent defendants are more likely to be detained than defendants who can afford an attorney. Second, indigent defendants

---

[38] R. Rovner-Pieczenik, A. Rapoport, & M. Lane, How Does Your Defender Office Rate? Self-Evaluation Manual for Public Defender Offices (1977), especially pages 38-43 concerning measures of "attorney competence." American Bar Association Project on Standards for Criminal Justice, Standards Relating to the Prosecution Function and the Defense Function (1971), especially pages 225-228 concerning the "duty to investigate." Genego, *Future of Effective Assistance of Counsel: Performance Standards and Complete Representation*, 22 American Criminal Law Review 181 (Fall 1984). National Legal Aid and Defender Association, National Study Commission on Defense Services, Guidelines for Legal Defense System in the United States (1976), especially pages 428-447 on "ensuring effectiveness."

[39] *See, e.g.*, R. Hermann, E. Single & J. Boston, Counsel for the Poor: Criminal Defense in Urban America (1977); Sterling, *Retained Counsel Versus the Public Defender*, in The defense Counsel (W.F. McDonald ed. 1983); Willison, *The Effects of Counsel on the Severity of Criminal Sentences: A Statistical Assessment*, 9 Justice System Journal 87 (1984).

are more likely to have prior records that will be influential at sentencing. Third, indigent defendants are thought to be less assertive of their rights than defendants who can afford to pay for attorneys.[40]

Both of these approaches contribute to the assessment of defense counsel. The first approach is appropriate for examining work that individual attorneys put into specific cases, but it provides no measure of what the attorney accomplishes. Certainly, an attorney may meet with the client, interview witnesses, and research the law, but do none of these activities effectively. The second approach, which examines outcomes, is used in this study. It permits a blunt but important comparison concerning the performance of groups of attorneys, is measurable, and is of utmost concern to defendants. Undoubtedly, there are limitations to the second approach because of the bluntness of available measures of performance. Attention needs to be paid to developing more-refined indicators of the quality of performance.

Conviction Rates

A fundamental concern to criminal defendants is gaining an acquittal or a dismissal. With a conviction comes the imposition of penalties. One basic goal of the defense attorney is to minimize the possibility of criminal penalties. In measuring this goal, the standard is that the lower the conviction rate for a given set of defense attorneys, the more successful they are in gaining favorable outcomes for their clients.

Indigent defenders perform as well as privately retained counsel in meeting this standard under a wide range of conditions (see **Table 14**). The conviction rates of defendants represented by public defenders, contract attorneys, assigned counsel, and privately retained counsel, when all nine courts are combined, are strikingly similar. Public defenders have a conviction rate of 84.4 percent, contract attorneys have a rate of 83.6 percent, assigned counsel have a rate of 85.3 percent, and privately retained counsel have a rate of 83.4 percent. There is no statistically significant difference among these rates. Defendants are no worse off with one type of defense attorney than another, which means that defendants with privately retained counsel do no better, or worse, on average, than do indigent defendants with a publicly appointed attorney.[41]

---

[40] Willison, *supra* note 39, at 88, claims that empirical studies show that favorable outcomes depend on the characteristics of defendants and not the type of counsel. He says that indigent defense counsel, therefore, will not perform as well as privately retained counsel even if they are adequately funded or have workable caseloads, "so long as they continue to represent disadvantaged defendants facing serious criminal charges and possessing extensive criminal records."

[41] In this chapter, two basic statistical tests are applied to determine whether there is a connection between the different types of defense attorneys and performance and the strength of the connection. The first test

Chapter IV Performance and Indigent Defense

Table 14
Are Defendants Represented by Indigent Defenders More Likely to Be Convicted than Defendants Represented by Privately Retained Counsel?
Felony Dispositions from Nine General Jurisdiction Courts

	Public Defenders	Contract Attorneys	Assigned Attorneys	Privately Retained Counsel
Acquittal, Dismissal	15.6%	16.4%	14.7%	16.6%
	(185)	(35)	(127)	(98)
Conviction	84.4%	83.6%	85.3%	83.4%
	(998)	(179)	(739)	(492)

Chi-Square = 1.26   Significance Level = .77   Cramer's V = .02

The similarity in the conviction rates among the different types of defense attorneys extends to cases that go to trial. Indigent defenders are no less successful in gaining acquittals or dismissals for their clients than are privately retained counsel (see **Table 15**). There is no statistically significant relationship between the types of attorneys and the likelihood of conviction at trial.

The results in Tables 14 and 15 raise an additional question. Are the conviction rates similar for different types of attorneys in both the large and small courts? This more refined question outstrips the available data to some extent. There are too few contract attorneys in either the large or small courts to permit valid statistical testing. However, if all the indigent defenders are collapsed into one category, then this question can be addressed in terms of the conviction rates of publicly appointed attorneys versus privately retained counsel.

There is no linkage between the type of attorney and the likelihood of conviction either in the large or in the small courts (see **Table 16**). The conviction rates for publicly appointed and the privately retained attorneys in the large courts

---

is a test of significance. The test of significance indicates whether there is a systematic connection as opposed to a coincidental connection. The chi-square test is applied. This technique generates a number and a corresponding level of significance. The smaller the significance level, the less likely the observed pattern could have happened by chance alone. In this report, the benchmark of .01 is used (i.e., results could have happened by chance alone 1 time out of a 100). In all of the tables, the chi-square value and the level at which it is significant are reported.

The second test is called a test of association. If there is a systematic connection, how close is it? The test of association measures the strength of connection in terms of a correlation coefficient. The coefficient ranges in value from zero to one. The larger the value of the coefficient, the tighter the connection between the different types of attorneys and various case outcomes. That is, the result is more meaningful because the connections between the variables are stronger. The phi-square and the Cramer's V correlations are the tests of association that are applied. Phi-square is appropriate for all two-by-two tables and Cramer's V is appropriate for the others. Finally, the rule of thumb is that coefficients below .20 indicate weak connections between the types of attorneys and case outcomes, those from .21 to .40 indicate moderate connections, and coefficients from .41 to 1.0 indicate strong connections.

Table 15
At Trial, Are Privately Retained Counsel More Successful than Indigent Defenders?
Felony Dispositions from Nine General Jurisdiction Courts

	Public Defenders	Contract Attorneys	Assigned Counsel	Privately Retained Counsel
Acquittal, Dismissal	23.2% (28)	28.6% (4)	33.3% (34)	25.6% (21)
Conviction	76.3% (90)	71.4% (10)	66.7% (68)	74.4% (61)

Chi-Square = 2.74   Significance Level = .43   Cramer's V = .09

Table 16
Do Privately Retained Counsel Have Lower Conviction Rates in Different Sized Courts?
Felony Dispositions in Five Large Courts
(Detroit, Seattle, Denver, Norfolk, and Monterey)

	Publicly Appointed	Privately Retained
Acquittal, Dismissal	15.2% (290)	18.0% (72)
Conviction	84.8% (1614)	82.0% (328)

Chi-Square = 1.91   Significance Level = .17   Phi-Square = .03

Felony Dispositions in Four Small Courts
(Oxford, Globe, Island, and San Juan)

	Publicly Appointed	Privately Retained
Acquittal, Dismissal	15.9% (57)	13.7% (26)
Conviction	84.1% (302)	86.3% (164)

Chi-Square = .46   Significance Level = .49   Phi-Square = .03

are 84.8 percent and 82 percent, respectively. In the small courts, the parallel percentages are 84.1 and 86.3. These are not statistically significant differences. Hence, within the limitations of the available data, the evidence indicates that

Table 17
Do Privately Retained Counsel Gain More Charge Reductions than Indigent Defenders in Cases Disposed of by Guilty Pleas?
Felony Dispositions from Nine General Jurisdiction Courts

	Public Defenders	Contract Attorneys	Assigned Counsel	Privately Retained Counsel
Convicted on Reduced Charge	25.7% (233)	50.9% (86)	26.4% (177)	31.9% (137)
Convicted on Same Charge	74.3% (675)	49.1% (83)	73.6% (494)	68.1% (293)

Chi-Square = 48.12   Significance Level = .0001   Cramer's V = .15

indigent defenders do as well as privately retained counsel in terms of a fundamental criterion of performance. The likelihood of an indigent defendant being convicted is not influenced significantly by the fact that the defense attorney is publicly appointed.[42]

Charge Reductions

From the perspective of the defendant and the defense attorney, any success is a big victory. However, most defendants are convicted; thus, another important outcome that most defendants strive for is a reduction in the seriousness of charge. If the offense at conviction is a less serious offense than the offense with which the defendant was initially charged, this outcome is favorable to the defendant. The performance question, therefore, is do indigent defenders have significantly different charge reduction rates from those of privately retained counsel?

For the four types of defense attorneys, this question can be addressed only for the cases disposed of by guilty pleas because the number of trials is limited for some categories of attorneys. The data reveal that there are significant differences in charge reduction rates across the categories of defense attorneys. The charge reduction rates for public defenders, contract attorneys, assigned counsel, and privately retained counsel are 25.7, 50.9, 26.4, and 31.9 percent, respectively (see **Table 17**). Contract

---

[42] There are too few cases to determine if the conviction rates for the four types of defense vary by type of offense. However, it is possible to compare all publicly appointed counsel with privately retained counsel for each of the four broad offense categories (crimes against the person, drug sale/possession, burglary/theft, and other types of felonies). The results indicate that there are no statistically significant differences between the conviction rates of public and private defense counsel for any of the offense categories.

Table 18
Do Privately Retained Counsel Gain More Charge Reductions than Publicly Appointed Attorneys?
Felony Dispositions from Five Large Courts
(Detroit, Seattle, Denver, Norfolk, and Monterey)

	Publicly Appointed	Privately Retained
Convicted on Reduced Charge	26.3% (425)	32.0% (105)
Convicted on Same Charge	73.7% (1189)	68.0% (223)

Chi-Square = 4.43   Significance Level = .04   Phi-Square = .05

Felony Dispositions from Four Small Courts
(Oxford, Globe, Island, and San Juan)

	Publicly Appointed	Privately Retained
Convicted on Reduced Charge	37.4% (113)	28.7% (47)
Convicted on Same Charge	62.6% (189)	71.3% (117)

Chi-Square = 3.62   Significance Level = .06   Phi-Square = .05

attorneys do considerably better than the privately retained counsel, who do slightly better than the public defenders or the assigned counsel.[43] Hence, for cases involving guilty pleas, there are mixed results concerning the performance of indigent defenders. Some indigent defenders perform quite well, whereas others perform less well than privately retained counsel.

If all indigent defenders are collapsed into one category, then the question of the link between type of attorney and charge reductions also can be examined for different sized courts. The size of the court produces opposite effects (see **Table 18**). In the large courts, privately retained attorneys gain more reductions (32 percent) than do publicly appointed counsel (26.3 percent). In the small courts, privately retained counsel gain fewer reductions (28.7 percent) than do publicly appointed counsel (37.4 percent). Both sets of results are weak statistically, however. In the large courts, the correlation between the type of attorney and the likelihood of a charge reduction is very low (phi-square = .05). For the small courts, the relationship is not statistically significant. Hence, while the type of defense attorney may have some effect on charge reductions, the effect is negligible.

---

[43] The relatively high level of success among contract attorneys may be due to the unusually high level of experience, especially among the contract attorneys in Monterey and Globe. See Chapter II.

Table 19
Are Privately Retained Counsel More Successful than Indigent Defenders in Keeping their Clients out of Jail or Prison?
Felony Dispositions from Nine General Jurisdiction Courts

	Public Defenders	Contract Attorneys	Assigned Counsel	Privately Retained Counsel
Incarceration	78.2%	74.6%	60.3%	57.1%
	(708)	(126)	(652)	(237)
Nonincarceration	21.8%	25.4%	39.7%	42.9%
	(197)	(43)	(259)	(178)

Chi-Square = 87.79   Significance Level = .0001   Cramer's V = .20

Based on these data, the performance of indigent defenders in gaining charge reductions is somewhat mixed. Contract attorneys do better than privately retained counsel, while public defenders and assigned counsel do less well. This connection, however, is weak statistically (Cramer's V =.15). Similarly, publicly appointed counsel gain more charge reductions in small courts and fewer charge reductions in large courts than do privately retained counsel. These connections, while demonstrating opposite effects, are weak. Thus, overall, indigent defenders perform about as well as privately retained counsel in obtaining charge reductions.

Incarceration Rates

The potential advantage that privately retained counsel have over indigent defenders should be the greatest in determining whether a convicted defendant is incarcerated or sentenced to probation, given community service, or fined. The prior record of the defendant is likely to play a major role in this decision. Unfortunately, the collection of data on the defendant's prior record was beyond the scope of this research. If it is true that indigent defendants are more likely to have prior records than nonindigent defendants, this missing information means that the examination of incarceration rates, without controlling for the effects of prior record, is tipped somewhat in favor of privately retained counsel. Yet, despite this potential advantage, privately retained counsel are only slightly more successful in keeping their clients out of jail or prison.

The incarceration rates are lower for cases represented by privately retained counsel (see **Table 19**). Assigned counsel and privately retained counsel have approximately the same incarceration rates (61.4 vs. 58.2). Public defenders (79.7) and contract attorneys (75.7) are less successful in keeping their clients out of penal institutions. However, the association between the four types of defense attorneys

Table 20
Is the Incarceration Rate for Privately Retained Counsel Lower than for Publicly Appointed Counsel?
Felony Dispositions from Nine General Jurisdiction Courts

	Publicly Appointed	**Privately Retained**
Incarceration	72.4%	58.2%
	(1369)	(277)
Nonincarceration	27.6%	41.8%
	(523)	(199)

Chi-Square = 36.00   Significance Level = .0001   Cramer's V = .12

and the corresponding incarceration rates is only moderate (Cramer's V = .21). This correlation means that privately retained attorneys are more likely to gain favorable outcomes for their clients, but this advantage is limited. A majority of the convicted defendants represented by every type of defense attorney are incarcerated. The size of this majority is greater for indigent defense attorneys, but nearly six of every ten defendants represented by privately retained counsel are incarcerated.

How indigent defenders and privately retained counsel compare is seen more clearly when all indigent defenders are grouped together. The correlation between these two types of defense attorneys and the in/out decision is a very weak one (phi-square = .12) (see **Table 20**). The slightly better performance by privately retained counsel, moreover, appears to be due to the effect of public defenders on the population of all indigent defenders. Public defenders appear to influence the higher incarceration rate among publicly appointed attorneys. The question thus arises, if public defenders are excluded from the analysis, then what do the results look like? The absence of public defenders occurs naturally when the courts are separated according to size. Whereas public defenders work in four of the five large courts, they are not present in any of the four small courts. Hence, **Table 21** shows how well privately retained attorneys perform compared to publicly appointed attorneys in both the large courts and the small courts.

In the large courts, privately retained attorneys perform better than publicly appointed counsel. The difference in incarceration rates is statistically significant, but it is limited, as indicated by a weak correlation coefficient (phi-square = .17). The underlying reason for the weak connection rests on the fact that indigent defenders represented 83 percent of defendants and obtained 74 percent of the sentences involving some penalty other than incarceration. Privately retained counsel represented 17 percent of the defendants and obtained 26 percent of the sentences involving nonincarceration. Given that indigent defenders cannot choose their

Table 21
Is the Incarceration Rate Lower for Privately Retained Counsel than for Publicly Appointed Counsel in Large and Small Courts?
Felony Dispositions from Five Large Courts
(Detroit, Seattle, Denver, Norfolk, and Monterey)

	Publicly Appointed	Privately Retained
Incarceration	71.5% (1147)	50.5% (165)
Nonincarceration	28.5% (458)	49.5% (162)

Chi-Square = 55.00   Significance Level = .0001   Cramer's V = .17

Felony Dispositions from Four Small Courts
(Oxford, Globe, Island, and San Juan)

	Publicly Appointed	Privately Retained
Incarcerated	77.4% (222)	75.2% (112)
Nonincarceration	22.6% (65)	24.8% (37)

Chi-Square = .261   Significance Level = .61   Cramer's V = .03

clients, and privately retained counsel do have some control over whom they represent, these differences are much smaller than expected. Moreover, in the small courts, the differences are in favor of publicly appointed counsel although the incarceration rates are not statistically different. The incarceration rate is 77.4 percent for privately retained counsel and 75.2 percent for publicly appointed counsel, which is in the opposite direction of the advantage that privately retained counsel are expected to enjoy

Thus, privately retained counsel perform somewhat better than indigent defenders on the basic in/out dimension. However, the greater likelihood that privately retained counsel keep their clients out of jail or prison is limited both in magnitude and in the scope of the effects as indicated by the low measures of association. Additionally, in the small courts, privately retained counsel and publicly appointed attorneys perform at the same level. Given the assumption that indigent defendants are less likely to win favorable outcomes because of their prior records, limited ties to the community, and other social circumstances, the observed

Table 22
**Do Privately Retained Counsel Gain
Shorter Prison Sentences than Indigent Defenders?
Felony Dispositions from Nine General Jurisdiction Courts**

	Public Defenders	Contract Attorneys	Assigned Counsel	Privately Retained Counsel
0-24 Months	44.4% (147)	48.1% (26)	41.5% (86)	31.7% (33)
25-36 Months	13.0% (43)	13.0% (7)	16.9% (35)	21.2% (22)
37-72 Months	25.1% (83)	29.6% (16)	20.3% (42)	26.0% (27)
73 or More Months	17.5% (58)	9.3% (5)	21.3% (44)	21.2% (22)

Chi-Square = 13.68　　Significance Level = .13　　Cramer's V = ..08

differences between publicly appointed and privately retained counsel performance are less than expected. The results suggest that indigent defenders are able to overcome the potential liabilities of their clients to a very great extent.

Lengths of Prison Sentences

The length of prison sentences is an acutely important dimension of performance. While every penalty imposes costs on defendants, the loss of liberty is the most severe. From the defendant's perspective, shorter sentences are better than longer sentences. Generally speaking, there is no statistically significant difference in the length of sentences between defendants represented by indigent defenders and privately retained counsel. The pattern to the data indicates that indigent defenders do better for clients. For example, in **Table 22**, a smaller proportion of privately retained counsel gain the shortest prison sentences (0-24 months) than do any of the indigent defenders. Hence, although the pattern is not statistically significant, the direction of the pattern indicates positive performance by indigent defenders.

Summary

Indigent defenders have been assessed traditionally in terms of the efforts that they put into their cases. Do they meet with their clients? Search for witnesses? File motions strategically? Present the court with concrete alternatives to incarceration?

The level of effort extended, however, is difficult to measure objectively. Moreover, it is virtually impossible to assess the effectiveness of that effort without examining the results. Hence, the purpose of this chapter was to raise questions of performance from a different perspective. What are the consequences of the attorneys' efforts? How frequently do indigent defenders gain favorable outcomes for their clients? Are they more, less, or equally successful as privately retained counsel in gaining favorable outcomes? The evidence gained from an examination of felony dispositions in the nine courts is that indigent defenders generally are as successful as privately retained counsel. The conviction rates, the charge reduction rates, the incarceration rates, and the lengths of prison sentences for their clients are similar to the outcomes associated with privately retained counsel. These results raise three issues for consideration.

First, the results are helpful in identifying what aspects of performance are translatable into management information systems and what aspects warrant further research and development. The measurement of case outcomes seems sufficiently feasible and the results seem sufficiently meaningful to merit inclusion into the monitoring of indigent defense systems. Consequently, judges, policymakers, and others concerned with the quality of indigent defense representation should gather information on how well indigent defenders do in gaining favorable outcomes for their clients.

However, the measures of performance in this chapter do not speak to the issue of lawyer-client relations, especially the time that indigent defenders give to individual defendants. How frequently do they meet with clients? What is the average amount of time spent with clients? Previous research has indicated that the amount of time that indigent defenders spend with their clients makes a difference in client satisfaction. The more time that is spent, the more defendants are satisfied with their attorneys.[44]

Satisfaction should not be confused with productive work. Indigent defenders know how to husband resources and to gain the most favorable outcomes for their clients expeditiously. However, satisfaction is part of performance and deserves further examination. Future research needs to be conducted on this topic to establish more precisely what amount and what kind of time indigent defenders, within the constraints of their caseloads, should be expected to devote to meeting with their clients.

---

[44] J. D. Casper, Did You Have a Lawyer When You Went to Court? No. I Had a Public Defender (1972). More generally, researchers have found that the felony defendant's degree of satisfaction with the outcome of the case is shaped by the procedural fairness of the process. Procedural fairness includes measures of the defendant's views of the defense attorney, prosecutor, and judge's behavior (e.g., Did your lawyer listen to you? Did the prosecutor pay careful attention to your case? Did the judge try hard to find out if you were guilty or innocent?). Casper, Tyler, & Fisher, *Procedural Justice in Felony Cases*, 22 Law and Society Review 483 (1988).

Second, the results suggest that judges, policymakers, attorneys, and others are not required to choose between timeliness and performance. Evidence from the nine courts in this study indicates that as far as indigent defenders are concerned, both goals are possible to achieve. The fact that these goals are not necessarily in conflict means that the task confronting the courts is to organize an indigent defense system responsible to community needs and circumstances that achieves both goals. That task, which is neither easy nor obvious, is possible. However, the lesson to be learned is that courts have the opportunity to design a system where both timeliness and performance are attained.

Third, the evidence of positive performance by indigent defenders raises the issue of knowing what role resources play in achieving these results. What resources are available to indigent defenders? How are the resources allocated across different areas such as attorney compensation, training, and staff support? How adequate are the resources when they are compared to those of the prosecutor? These questions are the focus of the next chapter.

Chapter V
Cost and Management of Indigent Defense

Cost and Management of Indigent Defense

Introduction

The central question in this chapter is, What is the cost of indigent defense services in the nine sites being studied? The question arises because the right-to-counsel decisions by the U.S. Supreme Court do not address directly how or at what levels indigent defense systems should be funded. Moreover, there are very few previous studies that have gathered information on the resources that state and local governments allocate to indigent defense systems, how the systems distribute and spend the resources, and the extent to which the resources are managed.

This chapter intends to begin filling the void in our knowledge of the cost of indigent defense services. Cost analysis simply means determining the value of the resources used to operate the nine indigent defense systems being studied. Attention is focused on the interrelationship of three key elements: (1) the amount of direct resources expended (e.g., the number of attorneys and the levels of compensation, support services, facilities, and training); (2) the management of resources (e.g., how the indigent defense system is administered and supervised, the nature of standards and evaluation practices); and (3) the degree of parity between the resources of the indigent defense system and the prosecutor's office.

The rationale for choosing this combination of elements is threefold. First, the examination of how resources are spent illuminates the budgetary options, priorities, and the choices that are made. How the indigent defense budget is allocated within a jurisdiction also casts light on a broad range of issues relating to the expected quality of representation. Are salaries adequate to attract quality attorneys? Do all systems have access to funding for training, investigative services, and expert witnesses? What are the ways that the budget for conflict cases are handled?

Second, the focus on alternative indigent defense management structures offers the opportunity to investigate various monitoring techniques. Are procedures in place to determine whether cases are handled adequately? Management is important to ensure that indigent defenders are adequately trained in criminal law, that they maintain professional standards in the courtroom, and that they comply with certain procedural requirements for which they are getting paid (e.g., they meet with clients, there are no stand-ins).

Third, the extent of resource parity between indigent defenders and the prosecutor's office is a salient issue. Are indigent defenders on an equal financial footing with their counterparts in the prosecutor's office? Or is the indigent defense system underfunded relative to the prosecutor's office? Defense attorneys enter the field for many reasons—a chance to gain experience, perform a public service, and, increasingly, to fulfill career ambitions. While they do not expect excessive emoluments, they do expect that they should be paid as much as a state's attorney, whom they believe is doing comparable work.

There are many paths that an individual community can follow to provide effective, professional indigent defense representation. Effective assistance and equal protection for indigent defendants are possible under a variety of systems as seen by the fact that very similar outcomes are obtained under very different structural configurations. What is essential to achieve effective and professional representation is setting priorities—taking into account the constraints of a limited budget.[45]

However, the consistently strong performance of indigent defenders across all major categories (i.e., public defenders, assigned counsel, and contract attorneys) is only partially explained by the monetary resources available in each community. The emergence and growth of indigent defense work as a profession are also underlying explanations as to why defenders achieve similar outcomes while operating in very different systems. Hence, this chapter begins with a brief review of the literature in order to demonstrate how the concepts of professionalism and resources are related.

Co-optation Versus Professionalism

It has been nearly 30 years since *Gideon*, but the debate over whether indigent defenders are effective advocates continues unabated. Do attorneys paid by the state have the same skill, autonomy, and freedom to represent their clients as privately retained attorneys have? Serious doubts were expressed shortly after *Gideon* and continue to be heard today.

An initial wave of studies focused on the degree of success that indigent defense systems had in fulfilling the legal assistance mandate of *Gideon* within the organizational constraints of the criminal court. David Sudnow portrayed the indigent defender as shaped by both organizational imperatives and the pragmatic values of

---

[45] Limited resources demand that choices be made. An understanding of how each system actually chooses to allocate its scarce indigent defense resources reveals the factors and priorities that each system believes contribute to an effective indigent defense. The goal in this study is not to say how resources should be allocated; rather, it is to see how resources are allocated and, in the process, to outline the alternative strategies each system has developed to achieve its particular goals. A more prescriptive approach is found in a number of other volumes that provide detailed standards for designing and implementing systems.

Chapter V Cost and Management of Indigent Defense

maintaining smooth working relationships with both the prosecutor and the judge. Indigent defenders might begin their careers with the aim of providing vigorous, effective representation for their clients, but they soon become co-opted. Their adversary role is redefined to one of easing clients into accepting guilty pleas.[46]

Similar conclusions were reached by Blumberg who contended that indigent defenders not only are loath to disrupt the routine nature of the court conviction process, but are involved actively in a courtwide "confidence game" to maximize guilty pleas.[47] Defense, prosecution, and the judiciary are portrayed as forming a core group of "insiders," working together to move cases rapidly through the system. The insiders' joint concern is furthering "their respective career, occupational, and organizational enterprises" by disposing of defendants as quickly as possible through guilty pleas. The defendant is a secondary figure who is treated by defense counsel in a fashion that best preserves counsel's continuing relations with the prosecution and the judiciary. Hence, Sudnow and Blumberg reach the same conclusion that indigent defenders soon abandon all pretense of professional commitment to accused clients because of co-optation by the court community.

This traditional critique, however, is at odds with another theme in the literature. Jerome Skolnick argued that the quality of defense services is underestimated by Sudnow and Blumberg.[48] He contends that co-optation is misleading because of fundamental flaws in the assumptions underlying their analyses. A better understanding of the system is achieved by considering the public defender to represent a more general phenomenon, that of the "cooperative attorney." Skolnick contended that cooperation is not equivalent to co-optation. The experienced attorney recognizes that "the prosecutor has his concerns for administrative efficiency and public relations which creates a situation for the defense attorney to take account of the prosecutor's ability to offer his client a less punitive outcome than he might receive if he were to challenge the state." Skolnick stresses that aggressive adversariness is a "naive view of the practice of criminal law in the routine criminal case"; rather, cooperation through striking a plea bargain results in a decided benefit for the defendant in the form of a charge reduction and reduced prison exposure.

More-recent studies examining the structure, process, and organization of the criminal justice system also have concluded that Sudnow and Blumberg's portrayal of the criminal court is inaccurate. Malcolm M. Feeley, for example, argues that the expansion of trained professionals—judges, prosecutors, and defense attorneys—

---

[46] Sudnow, *Normal Crimes: A Sociological Feature of the Penal Code in a Public Defender Office*, 12 Social Problems 253 (1965).

[47] Blumberg, *The Practice of Law Is a Confidence Game: Organizational Co-optation of a Profession*, 1 Law and Society Review 15 (1967)

[48] Skolnick, *Social Control in the Adversary System*, 11 Journal of Conflict Resolution 52 (1967).

throughout the criminal justice system has increased the amount of negotiation (plea, charge, and sentence bargaining), while simultaneously increasing the level of adversariness. Feeley summarizes his argument of the impact of professionalism as follows:

> The trial declined in the latter part of the nineteenth century ... at roughly the same time the criminal process was undergoing a transformation from a lay-administered process to one dominated by legally-trained, full-time professionals. ... During this same period both pretrial procedures and the rules of evidence expanded in number and complexity. These various rules were designed in large part to structure and restrict the power to lay decision makers, but they had the effect of giving greater authority to lawyers who could then exercise their expertise prior to trial. And as resources ear-marked for criminal justice expanded, these professional decision makers had increased opportunity and incentive to use the pretrial process.[49]

The expansion of the right to counsel has made a substantial impact on the way criminal courts operate by increasing negotiation and, in the process, enhancing the adversariness. Feeley writes:

> [T]he presence of an attorney who is able to *bargain* with the prosecutor constitutes something of a substantial increase in adversariness. The attorney's presence replaces intimidation with negotiation, domination with exchange. The very terms *negotiation* and *bargaining* imply that both the prosecutor and defense possess resources, a relationship that did not hold in a great many criminal cases when trials were more prevalent but the accused was more dependent. [Emphasis Feeley's.] *Id.* at 352.

In this view, *Gideon* not only increased the rights of criminal defendants but also ensured the rise of indigent defender as a profession and held out the possibility of a defense bar on equal footing with the prosecution and the judiciary.

The emergence of the professional indigent defense attorney marks a distinctive trend within the broader evolution of the legal profession. These attorneys are enjoined to meet the expanding obligation of the state to provide competent, effective counsel to indigent defendants. This sector of the legal profession reflects the continuing specialization of the bar as it diversifies to meet the needs of a particular clientele. Indigent defenders constitute a young profession, but they possess the defining characteristics associated with more-established professional groups. Indi-

---

[49] Feeley, *Plea Bargaining and the Structure of the Criminal Process*, 7 Justice System Journal 350 (1982).

Chapter V Cost and Management of Indigent Defense

gent defenders tend to view themselves as a community whose members share a relatively permanent affiliation, identity, personal commitment, specific interest, and general loyalties.[50] The idea of a professional indigent defense community is manifested, furthermore, by the existence of membership associations, standards, and a self-administered code of ethics, commonly found in other professional groups.

Professional status is mainly attained when its members create and control a set of identifiable skills. For the indigent defender, the claim of special expertise aims at gaining recognition and respect within the legal profession. The special competence of the professional indigent defender is demonstrated by the empirical evidence presented in chapters III and IV: there is little difference between the performance of indigent and privately retained attorneys, even though the former labor under constraints not shared by the latter. In light of this evidence, what is surprising is the number of scholarly accounts that continue to portray indigent defense counsel as ineffective advocates.[51]

One explanation for the lingering doubts over the capabilities of indigent defense attorneys is the widespread belief that they operate with an endemic shortage of resources. The conventional wisdom holds that indigent defense systems are either underfunded or severely underfunded and that underfunding leads to marginal performance. There is no doubt that underfunding exists in some communites. But is there unambiguous data on resources that supports the talk of a national crisis in the provision of indigent defense services?

Two basic approaches have been used in prior research to assess the cost of indigent defense systems. First, there are estimates of national expenditures for indigent defense services based on aggregate data from each state. These data are used to describe trends in expenditures and to compare the various systems in terms of cost per case.[52] The results show a clear upward trend in the nation's expenditures for indigent defense services. For the period 1982-86, total criminal defense funding increased by 60 percent (about 15 percent annually), from approximately $625 million to $991 million. These figures represent total expenditures in the state courts on the provision of criminal indigent defense services (both at the trial and appellate level). Much of this growth in funding is directly attributable to caseload growth (and the resultant need for court appointments) of approximately 40 percent (about 10

---

[50] M. S. Larson, The Rise of Professionalism: A Sociological Analysis (1977).

[51] *See, e.g.*, McConville & Mirsky, *Criminal Defense of the Poor in New York City*, 15 New York University Review of Law and Social Change 582 (1986-87); Mounts & Wilson, *Systems for Providing Indigent Defense: An Introduction*, 14 New York University Review of Law and Social Change 193 (1986).

[52] R. Spangenberg, B. Lee, M. Battaglia, P. Smith, & A. D. Davis, National Criminal Defense System Study: Final Report (U.S. Department of Justice 1986); Spangenberg, Kapuscinski, & Smith, *Criminal Defense of the Poor*, 1986 Bulletin (Bureau of Justice Statistics 1988); L. Benner, The Other Face of Justice (1973).

percent per year).[53] Although the growth in indigent defense funding exceeds the growth in caseload, it is difficult to assess whether this has secured resources that are sufficient for effective representation.

Using these data, the most common method for assessing the adequacy of indigent defense expenditures is to calculate a measure of cost per case. A cost-per-case estimate is derived by dividing the total estimated cost of indigent defense by the total estimated number of cases handled by indigent defenders. The nationwide average cost per case in 1986 was $223, increasing by 14 percent from the 1982 figure of $196.[54] However, problems of validity limit these estimates for three reasons. One problem is that all types of cases and offenses are lumped together, which means that the variable mixture of cases (e.g., felonies consume more resources than misdemeanors) is not taken into account. A second problem is that the variation in the methods of disposition (e.g., trials require more resources than pleas or dismissals) are not taken into account. Finally, the cost-per-case estimates do not differentiate between alternative defense systems within a single jurisdiction (e.g., a public defender handles some of the caseload and assigned counsel handle the remainder). These differences need to be considered before comparing costs across different systems.

The second approach attempts to refine the cost comparison by examining alternative methods of indigent defense services in one or a few individual jurisdictions. The typical procedure in these studies is to compare the relative cost of public defender and assigned counsel systems. For example, Cohen, Semple, and Crew, in a study contrasting four assigned counsel jurisdictions with three public defender jurisdictions in Virginia, concluded that assigned counsel systems are somewhat more costly than public defender systems (average cost per case: $164 for assigned counsel vs. $149 for public defenders in 1980).[55] Although these estimates provide a general sense of the relative cost of indigent defense services, they are based on imprecise and undifferentiated data and, therefore, are not suitable for drawing specific conclusions. Similar problems of data availability plague most

---

[53] Other surveys have been conducted that collect less-detailed defense data (indigent defense expenditures include payments made in both criminal and civil proceedings) along with information about various other components of the criminal justice system. See, e.g., S. A. Lindgren, Justice Expenditure and Employment, 1988 (Bureau of Justice Statistics 1990). Although not directly comparable to the data gathered by Spangenberg, Kapuscinski, and Smith, supra note 52, because of the inclusion of both civil and criminal payments, these data indicate that state and local defense expenditures increased by 42 percent between 1985 and 1988. For the period 1979–88, state public defense expenditures grew by 235 percent, and local expenditures increased by 158.3 percent. This differential in state and local spending appears to support the Spangenberg, Kapuscinski, and Smith finding of a national trend away from county funding to full or partial state funding.

[54] Spangenberg, Kapuscinski, & Smith, supra note 52.

[55] Cohen, Semple, & Crew, Assigned Counsel Versus Public Defender Systems in Virginia: A Comparison of Relative Benefits, in The Defense Counsel (W. F. McDonald ed. 1983).

multijurisdiction studies and call into question the meaning and validity of aggregate cost-per-case estimates.[56] First, it is often very difficult to differentiate both the number and types of cases (e.g., felony or misdemeanor) being handled by each group of indigent defense counsel. Second, there is uncertainty about what expenses are covered in the reported expenditures: Does the indigent defense budget include funding for training, investigative services, and expert witnesses, or are these costs covered in the court's budget? Third, it is unclear whether the types of cases going to different defense entities are of the same degree of complexity: Do assigned counsel get only serious, high-visibility cases, with the remainder going to the public defender? Without fully differentiated cost data, cost-per-case estimates raise far more questions than they answer.

Measuring the cost of different indigent defense systems is especially difficult because no single system exists, indigent defendant populations are not identical, and the scope of representation varies. In addition, there are few, if any, published accounts by indigent defenders or their funding sources about how resources are spent. Therefore, it is not surprising that the value of much of the past literature on cost expenditures is limited.

A Framework for Assessing the Cost of Indigent Defense

This chapter examines the allocation and distribution of resources used to operate the indigent defense systems in the nine courts. For example, what are the amounts of resources devoted to different areas, such as compensation, support services, and training? These factors are directly related to the provision of competent counsel to indigent defendants, but very little is known about the levels at which they are actually funded in various defense systems. In addition, the patterns of resource allocation within each of the nine courts will provide a context in which to assess the adequacy of defense resources. Is some level of funding, for example, available for training in all sites, or is it nonexistent in some? Moreover, the analysis also investigates how resources are managed and some of the techniques used by the individual systems to try to maximize the productivity of their resources. This inquiry is pertinent because most indigent defense systems operate with tight budgets.

The data on resources and expenditures were gathered from a number of different sources, including published and unpublished budget documents, annual reports, contracts, and internal office memoranda that were made available to project staff. Data were obtained through the help and cooperation of the Wayne County

---

[54] *See, e.g.,* L. Silverstein, Defense of the Poor (1965); Singer & Lynch, *Indigent Defense Systems: Characteristics and Costs,* in The Defense Counsel (W. F. McDonald ed. 1983).

Recorder's Court; Wayne County Office of the Prosecutor; King County Office of Public Defense; King County Office of the Prosecutor; the State of Colorado Office of the Public Defender; the Denver Office of the District Attorney; the Monterey County Office of the Public Defender; the Monterey County Office of the District Attorney; the Virginia Administrative Office of the Courts; the Office of the Commonwealth's Attorney, Norfolk, Virginia; the Maine Administrative Office of the Courts; the Office of the District Attorney, Auburn, Maine; the Gila County Superior Court; the Office of the District Attorney, Gila County, Arizona; the Washington Superior Court for the Counties of Island and San Juan; and the Office of the Prosecutor in the Counties of Island and San Juan.

This analysis of resource levels and allocations is in three parts. First, an estimate of the total level of resources is examined by tracing expenditures on indigent defense in each of the nine courts for the period 1987 to 1989. Second, the courts are grouped according to the primary provider of indigent defense services—public defender, assigned counsel, and contract attorney. The allocation and management of resources is then examined both individually and comparatively within each category. The third section examines the adequacy of indigent defense funding by comparing the four public defender systems with their counterparts in the prosecutorial offices.

Gross Expenditures

The available data on total expenditures for indigent defense in each of the nine courts are shown in **Table 23**.[57] The information provides important background information and is suggestive of three general points. First, the total expenditures on indigent defense in each court tend to be substantial given the size of each community. Multimillion dollar budgets exist in all the large courts. This is true whether the defense system is structured primarily as a public defender as in Seattle, Denver, and Monterey or as an assigned counsel system as in Detroit. Even in the smaller courts, it is not uncommon for indigent defense budgets to exceed $100,000. In addition, the trend in total expenditures is clearly upward. In eight of the nine courts, the amount of money going to indigent defense is on the rise.

Second, as the amount of money going to indigent defense increases, the need for accountability becomes even more compelling. Procedures are needed for two distinct, but related reasons: to describe how the money is allocated and to identify the services rendered. This information is necessary to convince the public and their elected representatives that additional expenditures for additional defense attorneys or support staff, for example, will be cost-effective.

---

[57] Because the cost figures are not strictly comparable, inferences should not be drawn about the relative cost of different structures of indigent defense. The factors affecting comparability—in particular the scope of cases handled by indigent defenders—demand more differentiation of the data and will be discussed shortly.

Table 23
How Much Money Is Spent on Indigent Defense?
Total Expenditures, 1987–89

Court	1987	1988	1989
Detroit			
Assigned Counsel and Public Defender	$4,892,914	$7,528,248	$7,290,557
Seattle			
TDA	3,690,371	4,292,520	4,758,882
ACA	3,291,294	3,581,519	3,888,047
SCRAP	1,208,614	1,676,001	2,199,657
Total	8,190,279	9,550,040	10,846,586
Denver			
Public Defender	2,095,785	NA	2,322,888
Assigned Counsel	432,082	NA	502,861
Total	2,527,867	NA	2,825,749
Norfolk			
Assigned Counsel	1,011,050	1,097,168	1,439,928
Monterey			
Public Defender	1,475,025	1,685,372	1,768,739
Assigned Counsel	81,895	177,042	150,647
Contract	101,250	371,250	371,250
Total	1,658,170	2,206,664	2,290,636
Globe			
Contract	109,952	137,890	177,420
Assigned Counsel	1,855	14,190	0
Total	111,807	152,080	177,420
Oxford			
Assigned Counsel	40,593	28,465	27,485
Island			
Assigned Counsel	145,471	201,794	228,301
San Juan			
Contract	29,790	32,421	43,715
Assigned Counsel	0	12,079	8,578
Total	36,540	44,500	55,293

Third, large and expanding expenditures indicate that the indigent defense community is not being ignored. It is becoming increasingly apparent to funding agencies that indigent defenders must be supported, notwithstanding some notorious disagreements about what is adequate support. Increasing defense expenditures reflect, among other things, rising caseloads, but they also reflect increasing levels of attorney compensation. This would suggest growing recognition that attracting and keeping qualified personnel is important. The trend, however, does not simply reflect a policy commitment toward protecting individual rights; it is also based on the prudential knowledge that the field of criminal law is becoming increasingly complex, with increasingly more stringent standards being used to judge the competence of counsel. The bottom line is that inadequate representation provides a basis for unnecessary and repetitive court appearances and for costly appeals.

Inside the Total Expenditures

The data in **Table 24**, while suggestive of important trends, say little about what each system actually gets for its money. To determine what problems an indigent defense system faces and how the problems have been dealt with demands a look inside the total expenditures. This closer inspection begins by grouping the nine courts according to their primary method of defense delivery: public defender, assigned counsel, or contract attorney.[58] The primary system in each court then is examined to determine how resources are allocated, managed, and what the different allocations imply about the goals of each defense system.

Assigned Counsel Systems

Table 25 provides a summary of factors that bear on the cost and management of the assigned counsel systems in Detroit, Norfolk, Island, and Oxford. This table underscores that even within a given category of indigent defenders (assigned counsel) there is variability among courts on almost every dimension. Differences include, for example, the method and amount of compensation (i.e., flat fee vs. event-based fee schedule), the availability of investigators and expert witnesses, access to a library, and methods of cost containment. This variation offers a rich source of material from which to survey alternative choices of resource allocation and different management structures.

Detroit

Detroit illustrates the issue of the completeness and comparability of the cost data. Although Detroit is the largest community in the study, its total expenditures are not the largest (the combined expenditures for the three firms in Seattle are larger). The primary reason for the less-than-expected level of funding is that Detroit Recorder's Court handles exclusively felonies and high misdemeanors, while the total expenditures for the other systems in this study include the cost of defending all types of cases (i.e., felonies, misdemeanors, and juvenile dependency family cases). Moreover, in Detroit it is very difficult to differentiate and to allocate a number of important indigent defense costs that are grouped within the total court budget. The expenditure data shown in Tables 24 and 25 for Detroit are solely the

---

[58]This classification is used because the different structures of indigent defense create barriers that hinder a fully comparable cross-court analysis. For example, the different ways in which attorneys are paid (e.g., voucher vs. salary) makes it difficult to compare attorney compensation levels in all courts.

Table 24
What Are the Resources of Assigned Counsel Systems?
1989

System Characteristics	Detroit	Norfolk	Island	Oxford
Total Expenditures	$7,290,557	$1,439,928	$228,301	$27,485
Funding Source	County	State	County	State
Types of Cases Handled	All Felonies and High Misdemeanors Only	All Felonies, Misdemeanors, Juvenile, and Dependency	All Felonies, Misdemeanors, Juvenile, and Dependency	All Felonies, Misdemeanors, Juvenile, and Dependency
Number of Felony Cases Filed in Upper Court	18,542	4,884	119	114
Number of Attorneys	653	78	12	12
Compensation	Voucher–Flat Fee Based on Offense	Voucher–Based On Time Up to Statutory Maximum	Voucher–Based On Time Up to Statutory Maximum	Voucher–Hourly Rate, No Maximum
Average Fee	$627 Per Felony Case	$40/Hour Out-of Court $60/Hour In-Court	$415 Per Felony Case $296 Per Misdemeanor	$40/hour For Both In and Out of Court
Support Staff	Attorney Responsibility	Attorney Responsibility	Attorney Responsibility	Attorney Responsibility
Investigators	$150/case	Rarely	Available–$5,972 Total	Rarely–$183 Total
Expert Witnesses	Psychiatric: $300/Evaluation and $150/Court Appearance Chemist: $200/Evaluation and $150/Court Appearance	Funds Available but Must Petition Court	Available–$5,274 Total	Rarely–$1,993 Total
Training	Mandatory	State Mandates CLE	Attorney Discretion	Attorney Discretion
Access to Library	Yes Located in Recorder's Court	Yes Court Library	Yes Court Library	Yes Court Library
Cost Containment Eligibility Screening	Yes Conducted by Screening Unit in Court	Judge Appoints	Screened by Administrator	Judge Appoints
Eligibility Criteria	Written Policy	No Formal Requirements	No Formal Requirements	No Formal Requirements
Partial Contribution by Indigents	Yes	Minimal	Yes	Minimal

Table 25
What Was the Average Full Payment to Assigned Counsel Before (1987 and 1988) and After (1989) the Introduction of the Flat Fee Schedule in Detroit?
Average Full Payment for the 12 Offense Categories Used in Detroit's Flat Fee Schedule

Maximum Sentence	Flat Fee	Average Payment Before Flat Fee 1987	Average Payment Before Flat Fee 1988	Average Payment After Flat Fee 1989
24 Months	$475	$491	$612	$475
36 Months	500	555	545	500
48 Months	525	549	579	525
60 Months	550	569	588	564
84 Months	574	584	650	575
120 Months	600	601	662	615
168 Months	625	571	575	625
180 Months	650	631	579	662
240 Months	675	583	561	684
Life	750	748	722	772
Murder II	1,000	1,116	1,102	1,000
Murder I	1,400	1,494	1,241	1,550
MEAN	628	628	634	627

amount paid in indigent defense fees. They do not include (1) the cost of the substantial management of indigent defense provided by the recorder's court, (2) the cost of investigators and expert witnesses, and (3) the value of judicial time spent in assigning indigent cases to counsel as well as certifying and monitoring the performance of indigent defense attorneys.

The administrative office for the recorder's court (AOC) is the central location for Detroit's coordinated assigned counsel system. Tracing the path of a typical case shows the early and extensive case management that is employed. An arraignment is held within 24 hours of the time that an individual is arrested. At this proceeding, the defendant is formally charged, the date is chosen for the preliminary exam, and bond is set. Representatives from the defendant screening unit (DSU—12 employees who work for the AOC) interview all defendants to verify information relevant to bond and to determine whether the defendant qualifies for publicly appointed counsel. In addition, each case is reviewed by a pretrial diversion unit (11 employees who work in the AOC) to determine the possibility of early diversion (e.g., first offenders).

Following the arraignment and the determination of indigency, counsel is assigned. On the day of arraignment, indigent defendants are matched to particular attorneys and to the Legal Aid and Defender Association (LADA). The next morning, the assignment clerk telephones each attorney (attorneys must pick up all assignments within 24 hours or they may lose the case). For each case, the indigent defender is given a packet of information that includes a copy of the assignment form, a copy of the police investigation report, a copy of the report prepared by DSU (which includes a preliminary sentencing guideline workup), and presigned discovery orders.

The preliminary hearing is scheduled about five days after the arraignment. It is required that assigned counsel meet with the defendant at least 24 hours before the preliminary exam and submit verification of client consultation to the AOC. Failure to do so will result in a $75 reduction in the final fee. Hence, the system is designed to have indigent counsel assigned early, encourages assigned counsel to gain an understanding of the case quickly, and provides a strong incentive to attempt to get weak cases dismissed at the preliminary exam.

On completion of a case, the attorney submits a voucher to the voucher division of the AOC (one employee). At this point, the amount requested is reviewed, all case information is entered into the management information system, requests for extraordinary fees are screened, and the voucher is signed and sent to the county budget office for payment. The information system allows the tracking of cases as well as all payments made to all assigned counsel over time.

All indigent assigned counsel and the LADA attorneys operate under the fixed fee voucher system. The Wayne County payment system for assigned counsel underwent substantial change in 1988. Before July 1, 1988, attorneys were paid on an event-based schedule with separate payments for every court event (e.g., each hearing, motion, trial day) based upon the seriousness of the offense. Now attorneys are paid on a fixed-fee schedule based on the statutory maximum of the offense. Under the new system, an attorney is paid the same amount if the case is dismissed at the preliminary hearing or if the case is disposed of the day before trial (even if many motions and conferences were involved). Average fees have remained relatively constant from 1987 to 1989 (see Table 25).[59]

Not surprisingly, controversy accompanied initiation of the new fee policy. Lawyers argued that the shift from an event-based fee schedule to a flat fee schedule created an incentive for indigent defenders to plead their clients inappropriately. This cynical perspective is not supported in the AOC study. These results indicate that (1) there was no statistically significant change in the percentage of motions or hearings held, the percentage of cases disposed of at trial, the percentage of defendants found guilty at trial, or the incarceration rates following the change in fee structure, and (2) there was no statistically significant change in the plea rate, although pleas occurred earlier and the number of dismissals increased.

The AOC in Detroit allocates a sizable amount of money to selecting attorneys to act as assigned counsel, training assigned counsel, and covering the cost of support services. Each attorney must complete an application form stating relevant past experience, complete the recorder's court's own training program (the Criminal

---

[59] Detroit Recorder's Court, Impact of the Flat Fee Schedule on Court Proceedings and Attorney Fees (Unpublished, August 1989).

Advocacy Program) within one year of the date of the application for provisional certification, and be favorably reviewed by a standing committee of the court consisting of five judges. Attorneys who have only recently passed the bar or who are new to Wayne County are given provisional certifications. The standing committee reviews the provisional attorney's performance at the end of one year and decides whether to approve full certification. Full certification is maintained by attending required training sessions during the year. Certification is to be revoked if an attorney is (1) disbarred, (2) convicted of a criminal offense, or (3) receives an unfavorable review from the judiciary and a negative vote from a majority of the standing committee.

Detroit Recorder's Court Criminal Advocacy Program (CAP) was established in 1983 and is funded by a 1 percent charge on all vouchers. The individual sessions reflect issues directly applicable to practice in Wayne County. Meeting the annual attendance requirements for CAP sessions is mandatory for all private assigned and LADA attorneys.

With respect to staff support, assigned counsel must cover their own overhead. However, money is available for investigators, interpreters, and expert witnesses. For example, investigator payments have a ceiling of $150 per case. The limit on psychological evaluations is $300 with an additional $150 available for a court appearance.

Norfolk

In contrast to the coordinated assigned counsel system in Detroit, a less structured arrangement exists in Norfolk. Court management over defense services is minimal. In part—certainly as regards costs—the explanation for this fact no doubt relates to the sources of funds and the responsibility to manage them: these reside at the state level with the administrative office of the courts. Few resources are directed toward assessing the competency of assigned attorneys, ensuring early case assignment, providing early discovery materials, and offering training and education programs. Appointment of counsel is usually handled in the lower court (district court) and made from a list of attorneys maintained by the upper court (circuit court). There is apparently no formal process for getting on the list other than writing the court and asking to be added. The list currently contains the names of 78 individuals from a variety of practices, including legislators, attorneys from Norfolk's major firms, and virtually everyone doing privately retained criminal work.

Compensation is by voucher and determined by a variable fee schedule. At the conclusion of the representation, the attorney completes a form, indicating the total in-court (compensated at the rate of $60 per hour) and out-of-court ($40 per hour) time.[60] There is a limit on compensation depending on type of offense. The voucher does not require a breakdown of how the hours are spent (e.g., so much in-court for

---

[60] In 1989, Virginia's General Assembly Continuing Joint Committee studying alternative indigent defense systems recommended that maximum fees allowed to assigned counsel be increased by 20 percent.

Chapter V Cost and Management of Indigent Defense

Table 26
How Are Resources Distributed in Island County's Assigned Counsel System?
Expenditures and Selected Expense Categories for the Entire Caseload, 1989

Expense Category	Island Assigned Counsel	Percent
Program Administration	41,325	18
Attorneys' Fees	175,730	77
Expert Witnesses	5,274	2
Investigations	5,972	3
Total Expenditure	$228,301	100

motion, so much for hearing, so much for trial). The vouchers are reviewed by a circuit court judge, but approved vouchers are forwarded for payment to the Virginia Supreme Court. Norfolk does not maintain its own indigent defense database, so the court has very limited information on, for example, the number of vouchers submitted, the compensation per voucher, and the types of cases being handled by assigned counsel. As a consequence, there is essentially no information available on the actual allocation of the total expenditure figure in Table 23.

Attorneys must cover their own overhead, although funds are available for psychiatrists and other expert witnesses. The attorney must petition the court to obtain them; there is a list of psychiatrists who will do work at the rate provided by the court. Theoretically, there is money for investigators, but in practice, the attorneys seldom request or receive such payment. The Virginia Bar has compulsory continuing legal education (CLE) for all lawyers, but, other than that, there is no training requirement for appointed counsel.

Island

The provision of indigent defense services in Island County shows that the creation and maintenance of a coordinated assigned counsel system are possible in small courts. Island's control of indigent defense parallels that of Detroit. Island's appointed counsel system includes a county employee, who oversees the management of the program, and a lawyers' association, which oversees the "quality" issues and represents the interests of the bar. Island County devotes 18 percent of its indigent defense budget to cover the cost of administration (see **Table 26**). The indigent defense administrator is responsible for reviewing incoming cases for eligibility, documenting appointments and fees charged, and determining partial ability to pay. Attorneys are expected to see clients within 48 hours of admission to jail. If that does not happen, future assignments of indigent clients to that attorney are jeopardized.

Island County uses a variable fee-schedule-based assigned counsel system. Assigned attorneys handle all misdemeanors, felony, juvenile offender, and dependency cases. Currently, attorney fees form 77 percent of total defense expenditures (see Table 26). The major issue surrounding the fee schedule is control of the indigent defense budget. The momentum for change has two related components. The first component is the amount of the cost. Costs have gone up and continue to go up. A new fee schedule adopted by the county commissioners in 1988 raised fees substantially (e.g., up to $400 from $240 for "basic felony appointment"; up to $800 per day from $500 per day for felony jury trial). These fee increases are reflected in a big leap in total costs from 1987 to 1988 (Table 23). The second component is the unpredictability of the budget. When the costs for appointments under the fee schedule exceed the amount budgeted, the commissioners are faced with a midyear "emergency resolution" to appropriate additional funds to the program. This situation has led to the formation of a committee to "study indigent defense costs and services" and examine the possibility of a fixed-price contract.

When total attorney fees (77 percent) are combined with the cost of program administration (18 percent), this leaves only 5 percent of the budget for all other costs of the indigent defense program. In Island County, this money funds investigators and expert witnesses. Most of the attorneys interviewed felt that the availability of these support services was adequate. While there is no formal training requirement, Island County has recently adopted experience and caseload "standards" for indigent defense. They are based on those developed by the Washington Defender Association. Judges and court administrators believe that attorney performance is high and, in practice, the attorneys are far more qualified than the formal standards require.

Oxford

Oxford County depends on a wholly state-funded assigned counsel system. As in Norfolk, the system is operated with limited local administration. Those attorneys who wish to be considered for assigned criminal cases can do so by either contacting the superior court clerk or the criminal case deputy clerk in the district court. At present, only 8 to 12 lawyers handle indigent criminal cases.

Eligibility for assigned counsel is based on the defendant's income and assets, although there are no formal eligibility requirements. Assignment of counsel typically follows one of two paths, depending on whether the defendant is indicted by the grand jury or is bound over from the district court. For grand jury indictments, counsel is assigned by a superior court judge at arraignment. For felony bindovers, the first appearance before a district court judge is set within 24 hours at which time bail is reviewed and indigency is determined. If the defendant is found to be indigent in either the district or superior court, an attorney is contacted immediately by the criminal case deputy clerk. There is an expectation that assigned counsel will meet with the defendant within one or two days of the appointment. Because attorneys pick up the case files from the chief deputy clerk before seeing clients, the clerk can monitor the timeliness of the attorney's initial contact with the defendant.[61]

---

[61]Anytime before the disposition of the case, the appointment may be converted to a retained counsel if new information is disclosed that would affect eligibility. Oxford County is aggressive in assessing some defendants for partial repayment of costs of representation, and the clerk monitors repayment.

Selecting an attorney is done informally with consideration given to the attorney's experience, potential conflicts, and preferences. No appointments in homicide cases are given to inexperienced counsel, but a new attorney who needs the experience is often paired with a more experienced one. Additionally, particular types of cases are not assigned to attorneys who generally decline to represent defendants accused of particular types of offenses (e.g., sexual abuse).

Oxford County works on a vouchering system. Attorneys are compensated $40 per hour for both in-court and out-of-court work. This fee structure was set by the legislature. Criminal defense attorneys did not believe that the $40 per-hour compensation rate was adequate. However, because the hourly rate was raised from $20 to $40 in 1987, they thought it unlikely that another increase would be forthcoming. No upper limit on compensation per case has been established, although the judge must approve the voucher. The judges have additional discretion in setting the hourly pay—a judge may allow less than $40 per hour for out-of-court work. Once the voucher is approved, it is mailed to the administrative office of the courts in Portland for review. Finally, the voucher is mailed to Augusta for payment. Oxford keeps only very limited information on the cost of operating its assigned counsel system and the administrative office in Portland only established an indigent defense database in 1989. As a consequence, it is not possible to tell why Oxford is the lone site with declining expenditures for indigent defense.

There is no requirement for training or ongoing education for indigent defense attorneys. Although the availability of funding for investigators is tight, considerably more is available for expert witnesses (see Table 24). Still, over 92 percent of total expenditures go strictly to attorney fees.

Despite the lack of a formal training requirement and minimal access to investigators, the prosecuting attorney, criminal defense attorneys, and clerk of the court all believed that indigent defense counsel in Oxford were quite competent. Because most indigent defense counsel also do private work, there is the belief that indigent defendants are receiving experienced, qualified counsel. The attorneys stated that handling indigent defendants in criminal cases was done not for economic gain so much as for personal satisfaction.

Public Defender Systems

Accountability of resource expenditures is an explicit goal of public defender systems. Attributes relating to the cost and management of the public defender systems in Seattle, Denver, Monterey, as well as Detroit's Legal Aid and Defender Association (LADA) are summarized in **Table 27**. There is a good deal of consistency across these public defender systems, although there are differences in the levels and sources of funding. One striking area of consistency concerns the level of support staff: one clerical position and one investigator/paralegal for every three attorneys. In addition, salaries are roughly equivalent across the four systems. Furthermore, in

Table 27
What Are the Resources of Public Defender Systems?
1989

System Characteristics	Seattle	Denver	Monterey	Detroit (LADA)
Total Expenditures	$10,846,586	$2,825,749	$2,290,636	$1,861,292
Funding Source	County	State	County	County
Types of Cases Handled	All Felonies, Misdemeanors, Juvenile, and Dependency, and Municipal Court Cases	All Felonies, Misdemeanors, Juvenile, and Dependency	All Felonies, Misdemeanors, Juvenile, and Dependency	All Felonies, Misdemeanors, Juvenile, and Dependency
Number of Felony Cases Handled by Public Defender	8,193	3,100	2,500	4,118
Number of Attorneys	141	26	17	19
Attorney Compensation Entry Mid-level Upper-level	$27,000-$32,000 $35,000-$44,000 $45,000-$59,000	$29,000-$35,000 $36,000-$45,000 $48,000-$60,000	$34,000 $50,000-$53,000 $62,000-$65,000	$24,000-$30,000 $39,000-$45,000 $50,000-$55,000
Number of Support Staff: Clerical Investigators and Paralegals	49 51	8 10	7 6	7 5
Expert Witnesses	Part of Court Budget Up to $350/day	Part of Public Defender Budget	Part of Public Defender Budget	Part of Court Budget Psychologist on Staff
Training	Mandatory, Internal Office Requirement. Attorneys Start with Misdemeanors, Move to Felonies.	Mandatory, Internal Office Requirement. Attorneys Start with Misdemeanors, Move to Felonies.	Mandatory, Internal Office Requirement. Attorneys Start with Misdemeanors, Move to Felonies.	Mandatory Court Requirement (CAP). Attorneys Start with Misdemeanors, Move to Felonies.
Library	Small In-house, Access to Court Library	Small In-house, Access to Court Library	Small In-house, Access to Court Library	In-house and Access to Court Library
Cost Containment Eligibility Screening	Yes, Conducted by OPD. Random Verification of Indigency Claims.	Yes, Conducted by Public Defender. No Verification.	Yes, Conducted by Municipal Court.	Yes, Conducted by Defendant Screening Unit in Court.
Eligibility Criteria	Federal Guidelines, 125% of Poverty Line	Federal Guidelines, 125% of Poverty Line	Variable	Written Policy
Partial Contribution by Indigents	Promissory Notes Written, Moving to Use of Collection Agency.	Minimal	Minimal	Yes

all systems new attorneys learn the skills of public defense through formal training, working with senior attorneys and starting out with misdemeanor and family law cases before acquiring a felony caseload.

Seattle

King County has established the Office of Public Defense (OPD) as a part of county government. During the study period, this 13-member office contracted with three nonprofit public defender firms to provide the majority of defense representation: (1) The Defender Association (TDA), (2) Associated Counsel for the Accused (ACA), and (3) Society of Counsel Representing Accused Persons (SCRAP). OPD is a division within the King County Department of Human Services that determines indigency and assigns all indigent clients to the contracting public defender firms and, in the rare case of conflict across the three firms, to individual assigned counsel. OPD staff complete a two-page form during the defendant interview, which covers various aspects of the charged offense, whether an interpreter is needed, and the defendant's financial situation. Individuals are considered indigent if their total resources are less than 125 percent of the poverty line or if they are on public assistance. OPD has just recently begun random verification of indigency claims. An individual may also be found indigent and able to contribute. In 1987, $228,688 worth of promissory notes were written and $84,094 were received from clients. OPD is moving toward the use of collection agencies to increase the amount collected.

Within 24 hours of arrest, a defendant makes a first appearance in the lower court. The bail determination is made and, if released and indigent, the defendant is told to contact OPD. OPD staff members visit defendants still in custody after the first appearance to determine indigency. Within 72 hours of arrest, the defendant appears before the superior court for arraignment. At this time, a defendant is charged on the felony information, offers a pro forma not guilty plea, and, if indigent, reminded to contact OPD, if he or she has not already done so. An omnibus hearing date is also scheduled. Despite being informed that they must contact OPD, out-of-custody defendants occasionally appear without counsel at the omnibus hearing. OPD has begun placing a representative at the arraignment who will meet with the defendant immediately. This change should facilitate early assignment of counsel and reduce the need for time-consuming jail visits by OPD to in-custody defendants.

Once indigency has been determined, cases are randomly assigned to one of the defender firms based on the specified contract percentage. It takes about two days for the case to be assigned to a particular firm and about seven days for discovery and case files to make it to the firm. If the defendant is in custody, the contract stipulates that the defense attorney must visit the defendant within 24 hours of assignment. The contract also stipulates that counsel must meet with the client before the omnibus hearing.

The defense firms are paid monthly through OPD based on a prearranged payment schedule. The ways in which the total budgets for 1987 were allocated within the felony division of each public defender firm are shown in **Table 28**. The most noticeable factor is that while the proportion of the total budget going to salaries

Table 28
How Are Resources Distributed in Seattle's Three Public Defender Firms?
Expenditures and Selected Expense Categories for Felony Caseloads, 1987*

Expense Category	Associated Counsel for the Accused	Percent	The Defender Association	Percent	Society of Counsel Representing Accused Persons	Percent
Salaries						
Attorneys	$504,475	54	$573,606	50	$157,298	54
Support Staff	164,100	18	236,922	20	47,322	16
Total	668,575	72	810,528	70	204,620	70
Benefits	152,048	16	179,419	15	35,923	12
Total Personnel	820,623	88	989,947	85	240,543	82
Office Maintenance and Operations						
Telephone	8,850		16,960		3,270	
Office Supplies	7,500		16,870		1,330	
Library	1,950		6,953		300	
Subscriptions	300		224		150	
Other	4,787		23,057		5,545	
Total	22,387	3	64,064	6	10,595	4
Training	4,185	0.5	9,165	0.8	475	0.2
Travel	1,390	0.1	1,863	0.1	2,050	0.7
Other Professional Expenses	2,100	0.2	2,201	0.2	960	0.3
All Other Expenses	79,225	8	92,430	8	38,088	13
Total Expenditures	929,910	99.8	1,159,670	100.1	292,711	100.2

* These data include the cost of internal office administration, but do not include the cost of the Office of Public Defense.

is very close (70-72 percent), there is a slight discrepancy in benefits (12-16 percent). Another point is that there appear to be some economies of scale associated with increasing size. The two larger defender firms (TDA and ACA) both spend 8 percent of their budget on the fixed costs of rent, capital improvements, and general insurance, while these same costs make up 13 percent of SCRAP's budget. (These costs are grouped together as "all other expenses" on Table 28). The result is that SCRAP has less money to allocate to personnel costs and, as a consequence, offers its employees a lower benefit package.

All three firms have orientation programs for new employees, allow new attorneys to "second chair" cases, and have ongoing training programs in place. Typically, the new attorneys in all three firms begin by handling juvenile or misdemeanor cases before moving into the felony division. TDA spends slightly more money on training, although the allocation is less than 1 percent in all three firms (see Table 28). TDA employs a full-time training coordinator who holds approximately three lecture or demonstration sessions per month and conducts two weeklong trial advocacy programs per year for newer lawyers. ACA and SCRAP use more informal methods, but the attorneys still have weekly staff meetings to discuss, for example, case problems and possible solutions, administrative policies, and recent trends in prosecutor activity. Investigators and social workers also have some training opportunities in all three firms.

The defender firms have no funding for expert witnesses in their budgets. Both the funding of and approval for the use of expert witnesses are controlled by the court. This open-endedness on expert witness fees creates a budgetary problem for the court. Moreover, some attorneys appear to be unaware that they may obtain approval from the court for costs in excess of the $350.

With three defender firms handling felony cases in Seattle, OPD is usually able to assign cases so as to avoid conflicts. If a public defender discovers a conflict, the firm is relieved of the case, and if possible, it is sent to one of the other nonconflicting firms. In some instances (e.g., juvenile gang activities), the case may be sent to an outside attorney.

Denver

Colorado has a statewide public defender system, in place since the early 1970s. Organizationally, the system is part of the judicial branch of Colorado's state government. The budget for the Denver office, which handles representation for the city and county of Denver, is determined at the state level. The Denver office also administers funds for compensating attorneys under contract for (1) conflicts and (2) overload. In 1987 the office had 27 staff attorneys and 8 contract attorneys. There are now 26 staff attorneys (see **Table 29**).

The appointment of counsel in felony cases generally takes place in the Denver County Court with the determination of eligibility made by the Denver public defender. Colorado uses federal guidelines for determining indigency, but the information that defendants provide is not verified. In an earlier period, screeners tried to verify defendants' information. It was expected that these positions would "pay for themselves" in preventing ineligible people from getting court-appointed attorneys. The savings failed to materialize, and screening was abandoned. A law effective July 1, 1990, requires a $10 fee to apply for public defender representation. This fee is waived for defendants in custody.

Total expenditures for the Denver public defender office in 1988 are shown in Table 29. Salaries and benefits comprise about 86 percent of the Denver public defender's total budget. Low rents and maintenance contracts in the Denver area have aided the public defender in reducing the overall operating expense. Moreover, using contract attorneys to handle most misdemeanors—at the rate of $2,025 per month—has allowed the public defender system to provide more-competitive salaries to those attorneys who are offered a full-time position.

Table 29
How Are Resources Distributed in Denver's Public Defender's Office?
Expenditures and Selected Expense Categories for the Entire Caseload, 1988

Expense Category	Denver Public Defender	Percent
Salaries	$1,547,844	74
Benefits	254,070	12
Total Personnel	1,801,914	86
Operating/Capital/Rent/Etc.	149,502	7
Travel	8,691	0.4
Contract Attorneys	135,678	6
Total Expenditures	2,095,785	99.4

Training in Denver has several components. First, there is a weekly in-house training program for all staff, generally with senior attorneys presenting the material. There is a ten-week rotation through the material (e.g., trial strategies, a session on closing arguments). Second, the attorneys have a buddy/mentor on the staff before whom they must "pretry" each case. The pretrial presentation includes practicing some cross-examination and closing arguments. Third, at the six-month mark, there is a one-week (45 hours) "boot camp," which is patterned after trial advocacy programs. The boot camp is deemed to be the most effective for individuals who have had some practical experience. Finally, there is a yearly conference of several days. The conference involves all staff, includes both in-house and outside presenters, and qualifies for 15 continued legal education credits.

Support staffing is determined by a formula set out in the budget (and funding is appropriated to cover the formula). The office is also budgeted a certain amount for expert witnesses. However, before receiving approval for expert witness expenses from the supervisor of the criminal division, an attorney must document and explain why an expert is needed.

Conflict cases requiring the appointment of outside counsel have been minimized through the creation of a "Chinese Wall" that isolates each of the regional public defender offices. Conflicts because of codefendants are seldom a problem because they are identified early. If the public defender perceives a conflict, the office asks to be relieved and that an outside attorney be appointed. Rates for appointed counsel were quite low in 1987: a maximum of $25 per hour for out-of-court time and $35 per hour for in-court time (after January 1, 1991, the rates were raised to $40 per hour and $50 per hour, respectively). The statewide public defender receives about $200,000 a year for overload. In earlier years, this money had been spent on appeals.

Table 30
How Are Resources Distributed in Monterey's Public Defender's Office?
Expenditures and Selected Expense Categories for the Entire Caseload, 1989

Expense Category	Monterey Public Defender	Percent
Salaries	$1,265,422	72
Benefits	358,027	20
Total Personnel	1,623,449	92
Office Maintenance/Operations		
Books/Periodicals	12,783	0.7
Psychiatric Services	19,013	1
Laboratory Services	4,111	0.2
Interpreter Services	1,220	0.1
Other	89,546	5
Total	126,673	7
Training	4,726	0.3
Travel	12,306	0.7
Other Professional Expenses	1,585	0.1
Total Expenditures	1,768,739	100.1

Starting in 1987, the money has been used to cover the contract attorneys handling the county court cases in Denver.

The office has a small library, but attorneys also have access to the nearby Colorado Supreme Court library and one located in Denver District Court. The attorneys use the brief bank in the appellate division. (Private attorneys do not have access to the brief bank.) There is no formal conference room; the attorneys use their own offices or the library.

Monterey

Indigent defense services in Monterey are provided primarily by the county-funded public defender's office. The public defender also has a grant from the State Office of Criminal Justice Prevention to deal with career criminals and receives state funds for handling capital cases. In addition, the superior court provides funds for co-counsel on capital cases.

Personnel costs compose 92 percent of total expenditures in the Monterey public defender office (see **Table 30**). Attorney salaries tend to be higher in Monterey than in the other public defender offices in this study. This is not surprising both because of the higher cost of living in the Monterey area and because it is an office priority in Monterey to hire only experienced attorneys. Typically, newly hired attorneys have worked in another public defender office, usually in a metropolitan area. Better-than-average compensation is a primary factor underlying the low turnover rate in the office.

The public defender office is small and located within the courthouse. This situation allows the public defender to minimize rent, but it also results in cramped office space. The budget for psychiatric, laboratory, and interpretive services is under the control of the public defender office and makes up just over 1 percent of total expenditures.

Training is a regular part of the office's operation, although it tends to be informal and is supported by a limited budget (less than 1 percent of total expenditures). There is an orientation program for new defenders covering office procedures and the local criminal justice system as well as regular staff meetings. Limited funding is available for local continuing legal education courses. The office maintains a brief bank and funds a small, but functional, in-house library.

Monterey County contracts with six attorneys, called consortium attorneys, to provide indigent representation in conflict cases. These attorneys are paid following the submission of a monthly accounting of case activity and must cover all their expenses (with the exception of investigative costs) out of the contract. They tend to be experienced criminal attorneys, having worked under contract for a number of years or having previously worked in a public defender office. Most of the consortium attorneys also handle some criminal cases privately.

When neither a public defender nor a consortium attorney can be appointed, some indigent clients may be assigned to private attorneys at public expense. In 1987 there were no formal requirements concerning attorney eligibility, the process of being placed on the assigned counsel list, and the level of experience necessary to take particular types of cases. The court has since clarified the criteria for appointment and which attorneys satisfy the criteria.

Detroit

Following a 1972 order by the Michigan Supreme Court, 25 percent of all indigent defendants are assigned to the Legal Aid and Defender Association (LADA), a private, nonprofit defender organization. The attorneys generate fees in the same way as assigned counsel (vouchers are submitted to the administrative office of the court, and payments are calculated on the same scale), and these account for the vast majority of office funding. LADA attorneys are not paid for each case they handle; rather, the money is paid into an office general fund and is used to pay salaries and office expenses. The more cases that are handled, the more money is generated. Hence, unlike the other public defender and contract systems examined in this study, LADA is not faced with the problem of handling an unknown caseload with a fixed budget.

Salaries and benefits constitute 85 percent of total office expenditures (see **Table 31**). LADA has a psychologist on staff, while funding for additional expert witnesses is controlled by the court. There is an office orientation program for new

Table 31
How Are Resources Distributed in Detroit's Legal Aid and Defender Association Office?
Expenditures and Selected Expense Categories for the Entire Caseload, 1989

Expense Category	Legal Aid and Defender Association	Percent
Salaries	$1,203,879	65
Benefits	373,222	20
Total Personnel	1,577,101	85
Office Maintenance/Operations		
Books/Periodicals	3,730	0.2
Other	262,161	
Total	265,891	14
Training	CAP	0
Travel	15,000	0.8
Other Professional Expenses	3,300	0.2
Total Expenditures	1,861,292	100%

attorneys, the chance for a senior attorney to "second chair" on some serious felonies and capital cases, and regular staff meetings. Ongoing education is mandatory under the court's policy regarding the Criminal Advocacy Program (CAP). The office has virtually no automation, so all case assignment and case tracking/management reports are done by hand. The capital cases are assigned based on experience and the ability to handle the case, while the noncapital cases are assigned based on work load. At any one time, each LADA attorney has 30 to 35 open cases.

Contract Defender Systems

Contract defense systems are the primary method of indigent defense delivery in Globe and San Juan.[62] In both courts, proponents argue that the contract model fits the needs of these relatively small communities. There is insufficient caseload to justify the services of one or more full-time lawyers, and the counties lack sufficient funds to sustain a full-time office (see **Table 32**).

---

[62] These are the main types when a contract system is used as the primary method of defense delivery. Contracts are also used to cover the assignment of indigent cases for conflicts and overload (e.g., Denver and Monterey) and as a method of funding, monitoring, and defining the scope of service of a public defender system (e.g., Seattle).

Table 32

What Are the Resources of Contract Attorney Systems?

1989

System Characteristics	Globe	San Juan
Total Expenditures	$177,420	$55,293
Funding Source	County	County
Types of Cases Handled	All Felonies, Misdemeanors, Juvenile, and Dependency	All Felonies, Misdemeanors, Juvenile, and Dependency
Number of Felony Cases Filed in Upper Court	504	45
Number of Contract Attorneys	3	1
Amount Per Contract	$48,000-$56,000	$34,000
Total Amount of Contract(s)	$152,000	$34,000
Budget for Conflict Cases and Assigned Counsel	$0	$8,578
Budget for Investigator	$25,420 (full-time)	$3,203
Expert Witness	Petition Court	Petition Court
Training	Attorney Discretion	Attorney Discretion
Access to Library	Yes, Court Library	Yes, Court Library

Cost Containment
  Eligibility Screening
  Eligibility Criteria
	Judge Appoints
	No Formal Requirements
		Judge Appoints
		No Formal Requirements

Partial Contribution by Indigents	No	No

Globe

During the period 1986-89, indigent defense in Gila County was handled by three contract attorneys. All of the attorneys handled a range of felony, misdemeanor, and family cases. In 1990 a fourth attorney was contracted with to handle exclusively misdemeanor and dependency cases. Attorneys individually negotiate with the county board of supervisors, which allocates the funding for indigent defense services through separate contracts. The three contracts were between $48,000 and $56,000.

All contract attorneys are experienced criminal attorneys who maintain private legal practices in addition to the Gila County contract. Three of the four attorneys have offices in Globe, where the superior court courthouse is located, and all must cover their own costs of office and clerical support. The board of supervisors has been fairly responsive in increasing the availability of resources to indigent defenders. Attorney compensation has gone up each year since 1986, and a fourth attorney contract was added. A full-time investigator was hired to work with the four contract attorneys, and travel funds are available for expert witnesses.

Once the terms of the contract are settled, management of the system by the court is minimal. Attorneys must submit monthly case inventory reports showing the number of new, pending, and closed cases; however, the reports are not checked nor do they necessarily balance. There is little screening and verification of claims of indigency and only limited attempts at cost recoupment. In addition, there are no formal requirements about meeting with clients, and access to discovery is left to the interaction of the defense counsel and the prosecutor. There are no funds for training and ongoing education in the annual contracts. If the attorneys pursue this activity, they do so at their own expense.

The indigent defenders believe that they provide their clients as much personal contact as their budgets will allow. For example, the contract attorneys send copies of all relevant court papers (e.g., motions) to their indigent clients just as they do to their retained clients. Dealings with the prosecutor's office, although informal, have become well established over time, and there are few problems with discovery and case files. Judges and court personnel agree that the contract defenders are experienced, professional criminal attorneys and that they provide a high quality of service to their clients.

San Juan

The indigent defense system in San Juan has been steadily evolving over the past 25 years and currently is structured as a contract system. During the 1980s, the contract was let on a low-bid criterion, with the attorney assuming responsibility for all criminal, juvenile, and mental health cases, including all overhead. The court exercised little direction or management, on the assumption that if there was a vehicle for appointment of counsel, then all indigent defense requirements were being met. There was general dissatisfaction among the bar and criminal justice community with the contract service. There was minimal accountability, with no monitoring of the contract defender's expenses, budget, or caseload.

Beginning in 1989, the court began to improve accountability in screening, verification of indigency, and methods of cost recoupment. Most significant for San Juan County was the mutual agreement by the commissioners and the court on three points: (1) beginning in 1990, indigent defense would be provided by a resident attorney, (2) attorney qualification standards would be adopted, and (3) a separate appropriation ($4,000) would be made for expert witness and investigation expenses.

San Juan is examining the possibility of creating a part-time administrative position to oversee screening and client assignments, to manage cost recoupment, to monitor the budget, and to process the payments. Management is believed to have the potential of increasing financial accountability and paying for itself through caseload and cost containment measures. Another alternative under consideration is housing the defense function in county office space. It is believed this would increase the number of attorneys willing to bid for the contract as well as providing a central location for client conferences and the administration of the system. The revised structure and management strategy are modeled after the Island County system.

Overall Patterns in Resource Allocation Across the Nine Courts

Three main observations can be drawn from the analysis of resource allocation in the nine courts. First, between 82 and 95 percent of all expenditures cover attorney fees and salaries and benefits. The ratio of personnel cost to total expenditures tends to be slightly higher than is typical for other public agencies and private, nonprofit organizations.[63] This suggests that the top priority in allocating indigent defense resources is to offer the most competitive compensation package possible in order to attract the most qualified attorneys.

Second, because the vast majority of funding is going to cover personnel costs and office-operating expenses, budgets tend to be tight for expert witnesses, libraries, and training and education programs. Funding for these areas exhibit the greatest variation across the courts. The primary reason is that there are marked differences of opinion between those who fund and those who do indigent defense work on how important these services are and what an adequate level of funding for them should be. Still, many of these indigent defense systems have been innovative in developing low-cost ways to meet these needs. The clearest example is training. Although indigent defenders rarely have the opportunity to attend national seminars, all the public defender offices have an orientation program, regular staff meetings, and more-formal office-training sessions that are managed and run by attorneys in the office. The Criminal Advocacy Program in Detroit is an example of how an assigned counsel system has funded and managed a mandatory ongoing education program.

Third, financial accountability and meaningful management can occur under any structure of indigent defense. Effective management systems include internal office control, as in Denver; a separate office that oversees all defense functions, such as the office of public defense in Seattle; or the administrative office of the court, as in Detroit and Island County. A more informal, yet equally effective approach to management is possible in smaller sites. Indigent defense work in Globe and Oxford is handled by a small number of experienced attorneys. The absence of formal requirements is more an indication of attorney professionalism than an indictment of the particular management techniques.

---

[63] *See, e.g.,* K.J. Chabotar, Analyzing Costs in the Courts xiv (1987), which notes that in labor-intensive government departments like the courts, personnel costs frequently account for about 75 percent of total costs.

Comparing the Resources of the Prosecutor and the Public Defender

In the debate over the capabilities and effectiveness of indigent defense attorneys, the most pressing concern is the adequacy of funding. This chapter has described the distribution and management of indigent defense resources in nine courts. This description, however, does not provide a means to assess the sufficiency of those resources. To accomplish this, one needs either a postulated standard or a relevant comparison group. Earlier chapters have argued that the most meaningful way to assess the performance and timeliness of indigent defense services is to compare indigent defenders and privately retained counsel. In assessing the adequacy of indigent defense resources, the focus remains on comparing indigent defenders with the most relevant comparison group. But what is that group?

Possibilities include a comparison with civil litigators specializing in, for example, taxation or commercial law or the select, private defense bar. These groups certainly have higher rents, more support, and a superior compensation package, but, more to the point, their work is very different from indigent defense attorneys. No indigent defender expects to make a personal fortune as an indigent defender; the compensation is known to be, for a lawyer, quite modest. Most of the attorneys interviewed said that they were motivated by professional goals other than money—the chance to gain a rewarding experience and to perform a public service. For these reasons, the most appropriate comparison is between indigent defenders and other public attorneys doing similar work in the same forum. This view fits squarely with a primary concern of indigent defenders: that their compensation and support services should be equivalent to what is received by their counterparts in the prosecutor's office. Both are publicly funded offices doing comparable work in the state trial courts. The extent of resource parity says much about whether indigent defenders are on equal footing with the prosecution and whether the indigent defenders claims to real professionalism are recognized and materially supported.

A comparison of the resources available to prosecutors and indigent defenders, however, is neither easy nor error free. There is often a "friendly" rivalry between these adversaries that limits the scope and availability of relevant data. As a result, this section provides only an exploratory comparison of salary levels, benefits, support staff, access to training, and levels of experience between prosecutors and public defenders. Public defenders are singled out because they are most directly comparable with prosecuting attorneys: both are employed salaried attorneys; have support staff and services covered in their budgets; and have all their resources as attorneys funded strictly out of public money.

Several questions revolve around the basic issue of parity between public defenders and prosecutors. What are the similarities and differences in funding for these two groups? What accounts for the differences? Do both public defender and prosecutor offices attract and hold experienced attorneys? Information addressing these questions is drawn from the three jurisdictions for which a public defender system is the primary method of defense delivery—Seattle, Denver, and Monterey (see Tables 33 and 34). To help improve the comparability, the analysis focuses strictly on the felony divisions within all three sets of prosecutorial and public defender offices.

Compensation

If the assumption that indigent defenders are underfunded is correct, one would expect to observe consistently lower salaries for public defenders. The experience of these courts calls this assumption into question. At the entry level, there is parity in all three locations. The public defenders in Denver and Seattle gradually lose ground, however, so that their compensation is relatively lower than the prosecutors at the upper salary levels.[64] This situation is reversed in Monterey. In that system, public defenders receive increasingly greater compensation relative to the prosecutors at the upper salary levels. The most precise statement, therefore, is that compensation levels for public defenders and prosecutors are close but that there are observable salary differentials. However, in these three jurisdictions, there is no consistent differential in favor of the prosecutor.

Staffing Levels

Given that public defender and prosecutorial salaries are roughly similar, another way of compensating for underfunding of the indigent defense system is to offer competitive wages to the public defenders and support staff who are hired, but to hire fewer of them. But with respect to the number of felony attorneys, this notion is not supported. Attorney staff size is almost identical among the three sets of prosecutor and public defender offices in this study. Public defender offices, however, tend to have slightly lower levels of administrative and clerical support. This pattern suggests that public defender offices are allocating their budgets to achieve parity at the attorney level (both in numbers and compensation). The tradeoff appears to be a somewhat reduced level of staff support. Funding for on-staff investigators is clearly highest in the public defender offices, with one investigator for every two or three attorneys. This statistic is expected, however, because the police department will do the majority of the prosecutor's investigative work.

Tenure

Another expectation, if the assumption of underfunding is correct, is that tenure at the prosecutor's office should be longer because higher compensation provides an incentive to make a relatively longer term commitment. This expectation is unsupported in that the average level of tenure is somewhat greater in the public defender offices in this study (see **Table 33**). In Seattle and Denver, the typical

---

[64] Currently, the county commissioners in Seattle are reviewing the possibility of adopting a uniform salary schedule for use in both the prosecutor's office and the public defender firms.

Chapter V Cost and Management of Indigent Defense

Table 33
How Do the Resources of the Prosecutor Compare to the Indigent Defense Offices in Seattle, Denver, and Monterey?
How Do Salaries and Benefits Compare?

Salary Levels	Seattle (1989) Prosecutor	Seattle (1989) Public Defender	Denver (1989) Prosecutor	Denver (1989) Public Defender	Monterey (1988) Prosecutor	Monterey (1988) Public Defender
Entry	$30-$33,000	$27-$31,000	$31,000	$30-$32,000	$24-$30,000	$24-$30,000
1-2 years	$37-$44,000	$34-$38,000	$34-$43,000	$34-$40,000	$30-$36,000	$35-$44,000
Mid-level	$45-$55,000	$41-$48,500	$45-$53,000	$42-$51,000	$36-$44,000	$46-$53,000
Upper level	$56-$61,000	$57-$60,000	$58-$69,000	$54-$62,000	$45-$55,000	$55-$65,000
Benefits as a Percentage of Total Expenditure	16	16	15	13	20	20

What Are the Numbers of Attorneys and Staff Support?

Salary Levels	Seattle (1989) Prosecutor	Seattle (1989) Public Defender	Denver (1989) Prosecutor	Denver (1989) Public Defender	Monterey (1988) Prosecutor	Monterey (1988) Public Defender
Felony Attorney Supervisors	4	4	1	1	1	1
Felony Attorneys	58	61	21	20	12	10
Administrative Asst./Clerical	27	21	7	6	7	4
Investigators	0	17	7	10	6	5
Special Services/ Paralegal	5	10	3	1	3	1

What Is the Average Tenure in the Office?

	Seattle (1989) Prosecutor	Seattle (1989) Public Defender	Denver (1989) Prosecutor	Denver (1989) Public Defender	Monterey (1988) Prosecutor	Monterey (1988) Public Defender
Average Tenure	2-4 years	3-5 years	4-7 years	6-7 years	5-8 years	5-8 years

public defender stays one or two years longer than the typical prosecutor. This difference is important because senior attorneys in all prosecutor and public defender offices stated that an attorney must stay from about four to seven years to allow the office to recoup the initial recruiting and training costs and get the "full value of an attorney." This somewhat greater average length of tenure among public defenders should not be interpreted to mean that the attorneys in the prosecuting attorney's offices are inexperienced. There is a distinctive group of experienced attorneys in each office: approximately 25 percent of the deputy prosecuting attorneys in Seattle have over five years' experience and in Denver, about 20 percent have more than eight years' experience. In Monterey, the tenure patterns in the prosecutor's and public defender's offices are very similar.

Training

New attorneys in both the public defender and prosecutor offices generally come straight from law school, and about equal numbers have worked in either a public defender or prosecutor internship program. Both groups usually begin with misdemeanor and juvenile cases before moving into a felony caseload. Given these similar backgrounds, it seems likely that the introductory and ongoing training needs of prosecutors and public defenders will be very similar. If training opportunities vary between these two groups, an important need is not being fulfilled. But in all three locations the opportunity for and style of training is quite similar (see **Table 34**). All have orientation programs for new attorneys, regular staff meetings, and some funding for attending state- or national-level seminars.[65]

The overall picture is one of an approximation of parity in Seattle, Denver, and Monterey. There is some variation in the availability of resources, but it is not sufficient to support the assumption that public defenders are severely underfunded relative to the prosecutor's offices, their most relevant comparison group. However, the conditions in these three courts are not universal. Detroit offers a different perspective and indicates that parity between public defenders' and prosecutors' offices has yet to be achieved in some locations.

There are several unique features of the Detroit indigent defense system that bear examination in comparing its resources with those of the prosecutor's office (see **Table 35**). LADA, a small independent "public defender," is not the primary method of defense delivery in Detroit, handling only 25 percent of the indigent cases. As a result, it may not have the ability to gain resources that is evident in the other public defender offices, which are the primary indigent defense providers in their respective systems. In addition, LADA's operating budget, which covers things such as personnel, rent, and office maintenance costs, is generated almost exclusively from voucher payments.

Attorney salaries at LADA are below those in the prosecutor's office at all salary levels. In addition, prosecutors enjoy a more substantial benefit package. This lack of parity, however, is a fairly recent development. In 1987 salaries at LADA and the prosecutor's office were nearly identical. Prosecuting attorneys received a substantial raise in 1989 (as reflected in Table 35); however, there is a good deal of similarity between LADA and the prosecutor's office. The level of administrative and support

---

[65] Training budgets for both the prosecutor's office and the public defender firms were also available in Seattle for 1987. They show an increase of $1,400 in the prosecutor's training budget between 1987 and 1989 and a $7,500 increase in the public defender firm's training budget.

Table 34
What Is the Availability of Expert Witnesses, Training, and Libraries?

	Seattle	Denver		Monterey
Training	Mandatory with a Budget of $14,331 in 1989.	Mandatory with a Combined Budget of $21,401 in 1990.	Mandatory Monthly In-house Meetings, One Week Program for New Attorneys, and Annual Off-site Retreat.	Mandatory Weekly In-house Meetings, Cases Must be "Pretried," One week Program for New Attorneys, and Annual Training Conference (15 CLE credits).	Mandatory Attendance At Office Lectures; Videotape Sessions. Some Funding for Courses Offered by State and National Professional Associations.	Mandatory, Primarily In-house. Budget of $3,500 for bar and State Professional Association Courses in 1989.
Library	Small In-house	Small In-house	Small In-house	Small In-house	Small In-house	Small In-house
Expert Witness	Information Not Available	Included In Court Budget. Up to $350 Per Day.	Information Not Available	Information Not Available	Information Not Available	Medical/Psychiatric Budget of $25,000 and Laboratory Budget of $6,000 in 1989.

Table 35
Comparision of Prosecution and Indigent Defense in Detroit, 1989
How Do the Salaries of Assistant Prosecuting Attorneys Compare with Indigent Defenders at LADA?

	Prosecutor		LADA	
Salary Level	Range	Number	Range	Number
Entry	$31-$33,000	14	$24-$28,000	5
1-2 years	$36-$41,500	30	$28-$30,000	4
Mid-level	$47-$56,000	38	$39-$43,500	5
Upper-level	$61-$65,000	48	$45-$50,000	5
Chief Deputy/ Defender	$69-$81,000	22	$63,000	1
Benefits as a Percentage of Total Expenditures		27		20

What Is the Level of Staff Support?

	Prosecutor	LADA
Administrative Asst./Clerical	47	7
Investigators	10	6
Special Services	13	2

What Is the Average Experience Level?

	Prosecutor	LADA
Average Tenure	3-6 years	3-6 years

What Funding Is Available for Expert Witnesses, Training, and Libraries?

	Prosecutor	LADA
Expert Witnesses Medical and Psychological Services	$20,000	Included in Court Budget: Psychiatrist $300/Evaluation $150/Court Appearance
Miscellaneous Professional Services	$20,000	Included in Court Budget: Chemist $200/Evaluation $150/Court Appearance
Training	Informal	Mandatory
Travel to Conferences (Budget)	$11,000	$15,000
Library	In-house: 12,000 Volumes with Annual Budget of $40,000	In-house: Annual Budget of $9,500. Access to Large Library in Recorder's Court

staff are similar. LADA has six full-time investigators, a librarian/researcher, and a psychologist on staff. While the average level of experience in the two offices is quite similar, there are some important differences. The Detroit prosecutor's office offers its attorneys a generous pension plan, with the result that about 30 percent of the attorneys have been with the office for over ten years. In contrast, almost all LADA attorneys work the average of three to six years and then move into private practice.

While the vast majority of new prosecuting and LADA attorneys arrive straight out of law school, the offices have very different training requirements. In the prosecutor's office, the orientation program is minimal and formal training almost nonexistent. They usually begin in less-demanding situations with limited supervision and direction. A new prosecuting attorney is likely to spend a day or so observing the case-screening process and the remainder of the first week assisting an experienced attorney with preliminary examinations. The new prosecuting attorney is assigned to misdemeanor cases or preliminary exams for about the first month and then begins acquiring a felony caseload. Because meeting the attendance requirements for the Criminal Advocacy Program is mandatory for all LADA attorneys, these attorneys have a substantial opportunity for ongoing education. The individual sessions are designed based on input from the local bench, bar, and police and reflect issues directly applicable to practice in Wayne County.

The inquiry into the resources of public defenders and prosecutors in these four courts reveals that there is a closer approximation of parity than the conventional assumption of underfunding suggests. There is no consistent resource differential in favor of either public defenders or prosecutors. However, the parity principle demonstrates its value by revealing what differences do exist and warrant attention.

Summary

Resources are central to effective indigent defense representation. Indigent defenders cannot be expected to resolve cases expeditiously and in the interests of their clients without adequate resources. This chapter has examined the amount and management of resources going to compensation, training, and support services, which are central to the provision of competent counsel to indigent defendants. How are resources distributed within each individual indigent defense system? What are the similarities and differences in the distribution and management of resources across systems?

The basic pattern across the indigent defense systems in this study is that priority is given to attracting and retaining qualified attorneys. Salaries and benefits make up the vast majority (82 to 95 percent) of indigent defense budgets. With such large personnel expenses, funding for areas such as training and expert witnesses tends to be limited. However, because training is thought to improve defender performance and lower the costs of supervision, many of the defender systems studied have created effective, low-cost training programs designed for both new and experienced attorneys. Another option, typical in the smaller sites, is to contract with or assign cases primarily to experienced attorneys with extensive on-the-job training.

The adequacy of indigent defense resources is assessed by comparing the resources of public defenders with those of the prosecutor. There is a close approximation of resource parity in terms of attorney compensation, training, and staff support in the three jurisdictions (Seattle, Denver, and Monterey) that use a public defender system as the primary method of indigent defense. Entry-level compensation in these three public defender offices matches that of the prosecutor. At higher salary levels, there is some divergence from parity with the public defenders either exceeding or falling below the compensation found in the prosecutors' offices. The greatest disparities occur in the areas of investigators and expert witnesses, with the prosecutors possessing more resources. Thus, whereas the performance of the indigent defenders in this study may be due to resource parity in critically important areas, such as compensation and training, this study reveals that performance may be constrained by the lack of parity in other equally important areas.

Chapter VI
Conclusions and Implications

Conclusions and Implications

Summary

Recent studies criticize the quality of the work by indigent defenders as ineffective representation[66] and of limited influence in shaping what goes on in the nation's state courts.[67] Yet, despite the fact that these assertions may be true of some indigent defense systems, they are not confirmed by evidence drawn from the handling of felony cases in nine state trial courts of general jurisdiction (Detroit, Seattle, Denver, Norfolk, Monterey, Oxford, Globe, Island, and San Juan).

According to the standard of timeliness, indigent defenders across the nine courts are consistently more successful than privately retained counsel in resolving cases expeditiously. They more closely approximate the American Bar Association's Time Standards for the disposition of felony cases than do privately retained counsel. Moreover, the speedier pace of litigation by indigent defenders can be observed even after taking the different types of offense and the different modes of disposition into account.

Is timeliness achieved at the expense of quality? When measured on multiple indicators of performance, indigent defenders generally do as well as privately retained counsel in gaining favorable outcomes for the clients. Simply stated, there are few statistically significant differences in conviction rates, charge reduction rates, incarceration rates, and the lengths of prison sentences in cases represented by different types of criminal defense attorneys (public defenders, contract attorneys, assigned counsel, and privately retained counsel). Moreover, in those instances

---

[66] McConville & Mirsky, *Criminal Defense of the Poor in New York City*, 15 New York University Review of Law and Social Change 582 (1986-87). The opening sentence of their volume-length, law review article is as follows: "Indigent criminal defendants in state criminal cases in New York City receive ineffective assistance from lawyers, who, for largely systemic reasons, fail to provide competent adversarial representation." From that point, they begin their criticism. However, for responses by the New York City Legal Aid Society to that criticism, see *Reply Memorandum of The Legal Aid Society to McConville and Mirsky Draft Report. October 1, 1985* and *Additional Reply Memorandum of The Legal Aid Society to McConville and Mirsky Report. January 3, 1986.*

[67] P. Nardulli, J. Eisenstein, & R. Flemming, The Tenor of Justice: Criminal Courts and the Guilty Plea Process (1988).

where the type of attorney does have an effect on these rates, the impact is very weak and not always in a more favorable direction toward the defendants represented by privately retained counsel. Hence, indigent defenders do not sacrifice the interests of their clients by moving their cases more expeditiously.

These important, but perhaps unexpected, results become more understandable in light of available resources. Based on the experiences of the nine courts, attorney compensation was given a sufficiently high priority to attract and to maintain experienced individuals. When compared to the prosecutor's office, the indigent defenders were reasonably close in salaries, administrative support, and training, although they lacked parity in the areas of expert witnesses and investigators.

Undoubtedly, there are limitations to the underlying data (e.g., all possibly relevant variables were not included), to the measures that are used (e.g., the indicators of timeliness and performance were blunt), and to the statistical techniques that are applied (e.g, the techniques were not the most refined). However, specific methodological limitations are offset by the general consistency in the results despite the diversity of the courts. The nine courts are different in their economic and social environments. They are organized differently, although their caseload compositions are similar. Finally, the courts illustrate the wide range of indigent defense systems extant in this country. All three of the basic categories of indigent defenders (public defenders, contract attorneys, and assigned counsel) exist in one or more of the courts. Thus, the consistent nature of results across nine courts with varying contexts enhances the validity of the results.

Indigent Defenders: A New Profession

The concept of a developing indigent defense profession may provide a deeper understanding of the empirical results. Broad patterns emerged from the interviews and on-site visits that helped to explain the performance of indigent defenders. Those patterns are as follows:

- The indigent defenders constitute an experienced cadre of attorneys. This phenomenon is most noticeable in the smaller courts where all or almost all of the indigent defense attorneys could be directly observed. The presence of defense attorneys with 10 to 15 years of experience is the norm in these settings. In the larger courts, the public defender offices indicate that felony attorneys, who are the subject of this study, are trained before they do felony work. Finally, the average number of years of experience in the public defender offices tends to be at least as high as the average length of experience in the prosecutor offices.

- The remuneration offered to indigent defenders makes their work economically viable. Whereas indigent defense attorneys must enjoy their responsibilities in order for them to continue beyond an initial training period, adequate funding permits them to spend several years in this line of work. The salaries of public defenders make their positions as attractive as other public sector attorney positions. For contract attorneys and assigned counsel, the revenue that they receive from indigency cases is sufficient to meet an appreciable portion of their expenses (e.g., overhead, secretary) with private practice providing the rest of needed income. The remuneration that indigent defenders receive provides them with economic stability, which, in turn, permits them the opportunity to gain satisfaction from other incentives.

The indigent defenders observed in this research possess the essential characteristics of a profession. They have both special competence and a strong service orientation, not just their own financial enrichment.[68] Their competence is shown in their knowledge of court procedures and practices, their abilities to negotiate the most favorable outcomes for their clients, and their success in knowing how to achieve favorable outcomes expeditiously.

Indigent defenders represent a distinctive subgroup within the overall legal profession. The service orientation and the special competence of indigent defenders are striking. This emerging professional character of indigent defenders puts their positive performance in context. Their ability to get the job done and done well reflects the broader development of professional indigent defenders across a range of diverse courts and communities.

Implications

The experiences of the nine courts have implications that extend beyond the boundaries of their jurisdictions. The nine courts represent a broad spectrum of the nation's courts, communities, and indigent defense systems. Hence, the following three implications are offered for consideration by other courts, attorneys, and policymakers across the country.

First, the results suggest the positive value of establishing an indigent defense performance management system. The system consists of three basic elements: (1) an explicit set of expectations concerning performance—indigent defenders should be expected to process cases in a timely manner and to achieve favorable outcomes for their clients—(2) measurable indicators of performance—chapters III and IV

---

[68] M.S. Larson, The Rise of Professionalism: A Social Analysis (1977).

provide multiple illustrations of how timeliness and output performance are measurable in terms of systematic data—and (3) the periodic application of the indicators to determine how well indigent defenders are doing compared to privately retained counsel. The rationale for the system is clear. There is a need to have a workable way to assess the delivery of services that indigent defenders render. Moreover, the system is suitable for use under a broad range of conditions, including a variety of both indigent defense and court structures.

Second, the analysis of the cost of indigent defense offers two important lessons. One lesson is that efforts to arrive at meaningful cost comparisons across courts or on a cost-per-case basis are fraught with difficulties, uncertainties, and hazards. Continued research and investigation along these lines, in fact, are of questionable value because a lack of a relevant standard against which cost-per-case estimates can be judged. Is the lowest cost the best? What is the threshold of minimally acceptable expenditures? The difficulties in answering these questions call the intrinsic value of the approach into question.

The second lesson is a more positive one. A potentially fruitful way to examine the cost of indigent defense is to compare the degree of parity between indigent defenders and prosecutors. This approach is promising because it provides a reasonable standard of comparison. The cost of indigent defense should be examined in relationship to other public sector attorneys who are doing the same sort of work. Prosecutors fit that description better than any other group of attorneys.

Additionally, an examination of defense and prosecutorial costs illuminates resources in key areas such as personnel, staff support, training, investigators, and expert witnesses. Instead of looking at an aggregate cost-per-case figure, the analysis of defense and prosecutorial resources will uncover in what relevant areas parity is approximated and the areas where there are sharp divergences. Judges, attorneys, and policymakers can use that information in making judgments on resource allocations.

The third and final implication is that it is more fruitful to view the structure of indigent defense as more variable and adaptable than the three basic categories of public defenders, assigned counsel, and contract attorneys suggest. It is simply not the case that there is a single, best category of indigent defense. On the contrary, policymakers, judges, court staff, and attorneys should choose that combination of organizational features that fits their needs and circumstances. The organizational structure that is good for one community may not be best for another. Moreover, the acid test of any structure is how it performs and that depends on how well indigent defenders meet expectations.

Appendix
*Profiles of the Nine Research Sites:
The Environments, the Courts,
and the Prosecutors' Offices*

Profiles of the Nine Research Sites: The Environments, the Courts, and the Prosecutors' Offices

Detroit

ENVIRONMENT. The population of Wayne County was 2,164,300 in 1986. The city of Detroit accounted for just over one-half of the total county population (1,086,220), making it the sixth largest city in the U.S. The total population living within the city, however, has been in decline since the 1950s. Approximately 39 percent of Wayne County population is identified as nonwhite. Per capita income is $10,681, with just over 14 percent of the population living below the poverty level. Wayne County's crime rate was 9,864 serious crimes per 100,000 population.

COURT. Wayne County has a two-tiered court system: first, the lower court is a combination of district and municipal courts that hears misdemeanors and traffic offenses, but that also conducts felony arraignments and preliminary examinations for all high misdemeanor and felony cases. Once the case is bound over for trial, it is transferred to one of two felony courts: Detroit Recorder's Court, handling all felonies and high misdemeanors committed in the city of Detroit (bound over by the 36th District Court), or the Third Circuit Court of Michigan (bound over by one of the other 25 district or municipal courts in Wayne County). Following a merging process begun in 1981, the criminal dockets of the two felony courts were formally consolidated in 1986. Since the beginning of 1987, all major felony proceedings for Wayne County, from arraignment through the sentencing hearing, are conducted by judges from both felony courts in the Frank Murphy Hall of Justice in Detroit. There are 34 judges (29 recorder's court judges and 5 circuit court judges on three-month rotations) to handle the criminal docket.

PROSECUTOR'S OFFICE. The prosecuting attorney of Wayne County is elected to a four year term. In 1990 the compensation of 203 of the 238 employees, including assistant prosecutors and support staff, was county funded with the remainder being "externally" funded (primarily federal grants). The prosecutor's office handles the vast majority of all cases in a "horizontal" fashion.

Most of the new assistant prosecuting attorneys arrive shortly after graduating from law school; they tend to stay three to six years and then move into private practice or, perhaps, the U.S. Attorney's Office. For the first month or so, the new assistant prosecuting attorney is assigned to misdemeanors or preliminary exams.

Attorneys are assigned to one of four divisions: screening; trials and dispositions; special operations; or research, training, and appeals. The first stage of a felony case is its intake through the screening and district courts division. This division screens incoming cases and issues arrest warrants relating to any crime occurring within Detroit. Once a case has been bound over to the felony court (Detroit Recorder's or the Third Circuit Court), it is given to the trials and dispositions division. One set of attorneys in this division, the docket control attorneys, attempt to settle as many cases as possible before trial. They work closely with the judges to encourage pleas by letting the defendant know that a plea at this stage will result in a substantially shorter sentence than a conviction at trial. If this is not possible, the case is turned over to the trial attorneys.

Seattle

ENVIRONMENT. In 1988 the Seattle primary metropolitan area had a population of 1,862,000, with the city of Seattle accounting for just under one-third of the total (502,000). Seattle, the 24th largest city in the country, experienced a growth in population of 1.7 percent from 1980-88; just over 12 percent of its population is identified as nonwhite. Of the nine communities under examination, Seattle had the second highest per capita income ($13,192) and the lowest percentage of individuals living below the poverty line (7.7 percent).

COURT. The Seattle (King County) court system has two tiers: a superior (upper) court of general jurisdiction and twelve district (lower) courts of limited jurisdiction. Until the mid-1970s, felonies were initially filed in the district court. This procedure was changed in response to the introduction of a speedy trial rule that imposed tighter time constraints on the prosecutor. Currently, only some minor felonies, expected to be disposed of as misdemeanors, are filed in the district court; almost all other felony cases are filed directly in the superior court.

The superior court has 45 judges and 6 commissioners. Fifteen judges are assigned to hear criminal cases with an additional 5 judges on loan from the civil docket. The presiding judge handles all arraignments and omnibus hearings; another judge handles all motions (and helps with arraignments and omnibus hearings if necessary); the remaining judges conduct trials. Judges are rotated annually on a staggered basis to hear criminal cases.

PROSECUTOR'S OFFICE. The King County Prosecutor's Office has a criminal attorney staff of about 85 persons (58 attorneys are assigned to felony cases). All office positions are county funded. Eighteen of the felony assistant prosecutor positions are fairly new, created to handle exclusively drug cases. The usual progression in the prosecutor's office is to start in district court, move to juvenile court, and then into the felony division. This process usually takes from six months to a year. There is a degree of specialization within the prosecutor's office: there are special units handling sex offenses, drugs, some arson cases, and some vehicular homicides. Homicides are handled by senior attorneys.

The prosecutor's office needs to fill approximately ten vacancies per year. The majority of new prosecutors are hired following an interview with the hiring committee at various law schools some time before graduation. The office also has an internship program. Approximately 30 percent of new prosecutors have participated. Interns and attorneys who have yet to pass the state bar examination work on juvenile and traffic cases. Roughly 25 percent of the current staff had been there over five years.

Training programs are available. About every three weeks, for the first six to eight months, new prosecutors must attend all-day Saturday meetings for training on a variety of topics. In addition, the office has extensive written standards and procedure manuals.

Supervisors assign cases to junior prosecutors. There are no office standards on the number of cases to take to trial, but the supervisors evaluate the junior attorneys' decisions in most cases so that "proper" case handling is instilled. Trial rates are examined at evaluation time, and any peculiar trends (too many or too few trials) are noted and discussed.

Denver

ENVIRONMENT. Denver is the largest city in the Rocky Mountain region. Its population of 505,000 in 1986 tends to be divided between a relatively affluent majority and a very poor minority. A most striking feature of Denver is its crime rate of 10,557 serious crimes per 100,000 population.

COURT. Denver has a two-tiered trial court. Felony cases originate in the county court; the grand jury is not regularly used. The general jurisdiction Denver District Court has 20 judges; 6 are assigned to felony cases. The court size has been stable since the late 1970s. The number of judges assigned to felony cases has not changed in the last decade, although in the earlier period the sixth presiding judge of the criminal division did not carry a full calendar. Before the intensive drug prosecution of the past few years, criminal cases had been declining as a portion of the court's total work load, a reflection of the declining population of Denver itself. In the last couple years, criminal filings have increased 16 to 20 percent. The judges rotate in and out of the various assignments, with their preferences playing a major role. Usually an assignment does not exceed two years. The current criminal division presiding judge has been in that position for three years. Each judge is free to adopt specific procedures, with the result that there is considerable variety of practices across the six courtrooms.

PROSECUTOR'S OFFICE. The district attorney is elected for a four-year term. There are 21 attorneys assigned to felony cases. Funding is almost entirely from the city/county, with some supplemental victim-assistance money coming from the city and state; there is no federal funding. The office has space in a new building near the courthouse. There is a library with computerized research tools and attractive conference rooms.

Attorneys generally come directly from law school. About 50 percent of the new attorneys have been legal interns in the office. The office is currently a mixture of career people and short timers, with a number of senior people with nine to ten years service. Attrition was represented as quite low, and staff positions are always in demand. Those who leave tend to go to small firms, some to the U.S. Attorney's Office.

As in other offices, most training is on-the-job. New assistant district attorneys start out with county court cases, graduating to juvenile and misdemeanor cases in the district court. It now takes up to three years to move into the felony division. This training is supplemented by monthly in-house sessions that attorneys are expected to attend. There is also a one-week program for new prosecutors put on by the Colorado District Attorneys Association. Once a year there is an off-site staff retreat.

Norfolk

ENVIRONMENT. Norfolk is a core city declining in population. It is losing both middle-income residents and some poor residents (through the demolition of housing projects).

COURT. Virginia has a two-tiered trial court—the limited jurisdiction general district court and the general jurisdiction circuit court. Felonies come to the circuit court by two routes—from the general district court as bindovers and direct grand jury indictments. Perhaps as many as 20 to 30 percent of the felony cases are direct indictments. This is potentially important since the direct indictment cases have counsel appointed in the circuit court; the bindovers will come with counsel appointed in the general district court. The circuit court has exclusive felony jurisdiction; it also hears indicted misdemeanors.

There are three distinctive features of Virginia's criminal procedure: First, the commonwealth's attorney is not involved in the initiation (i.e., filing and screening) of criminal cases in the general district court. A private individual or a police office can initiate criminal proceedings directly by obtaining a warrant from a magistrate. Individuals are encouraged to confer with the police in obtaining a warrant, but this practice is not required. Second, the prosecutor controls the calendaring of criminal cases in the circuit court. Third, the circuit court uses a variant of the master calendar: There are nine judges, with about half assigned to criminal matters at any time. However, assignment is on a daily basis depending upon the number and mixture of cases scheduled. The normal arrangement is for a judge to hear criminal cases Monday, Wednesday, and Friday one week and Tuesday and Thursday the next week. Each evening the cases set for the following day are distributed to the judges, and calendars are prepared and posted. As a result of the prosecutor's control of criminal calendaring, the judges may have limited knowledge of whether a case is a plea or a trial.

PROSECUTOR'S OFFICE. There is an elected commonwealth's attorney. The office is housed in a government office building (built in the early 1970s) across a plaza from the court buildings. Office space looked cramped (i.e., library and reference material stored in the hallway). There is limited computer support for management purposes (e.g., no information on pending cases, dispositions).

Prosecution of criminal cases is handled by an attorney staff of 18—a chief deputy and 17 others. These individuals handle felony prosecutions in both the circuit court and general district court, including juvenile cases. When the current incumbent took office, the city was persuaded to supplement funding, enabling the office to offer more competitive salaries (e.g., starting salaries jumped from about $17,000 to $30,000). The office has few grant-funded functions; those that do exist include an attorney handling child support (cases) funded by the state and a paralegal who works on drug-related cases.

Virginia does not have a law-student practice rule, and the office will not carry an individual waiting bar admission. Because no one is hired without a Virginia Bar admission, few deputies come right from law school. Rather, they tend to have some degree of experience—coming from clerkships, private practice, other prosecutor's offices, and judge advocates general. The upgrading of salaries has changed the character of the staff—more-experienced people are coming to the office and tend to stay longer, though there is always turnover.

The chief deputy assigns attorneys—to juvenile court, the preliminary hearing courtrooms, circuit court, and so forth. The office has vertical representation from the preliminary hearing. Thus, an attorney handling a case at that hearing will normally keep the case, although the chief deputy will review the assignments to assure some caseload parity. The general district court runs separate preliminary hearing courtrooms for property/drug and violent offenses, so individuals will be assigned cases based on their level of experience and expertise.

Monterey

ENVIRONMENT. The population of Monterey County was 340,000 in 1986. Approximately 15 percent of the county population is Hispanic. In 1985 the per capita income was $10,420, with 11.4 percent of the population below the poverty level. Monterey County's crime rate was 5,419 serious crimes per 100,000 population.

COURT. The county has two superior court branches: Salinas, which has six judges, including one who hears juvenile cases exclusively, and Monterey, which has two judges. The main court in Salinas serves the north coast and the inland, agricultural region (population 240,000); the Monterey branch serves the greater Monterey peninsula (population 100,000).

Felony defendants are charged by an information filed by the district attorney. For defendants arrested on the street, a prima facie case is presented at a preliminary hearing in the municipal court, and if sufficient cause is found to charge the defendant with a felony, the defendant is "held to answer" in the superior court, where the information is filed. At the preliminary hearing, the defendant receives a statement of rights, probable cause is determined, bail is set, and an attorney is assigned. The defendant can waive the preliminary hearing and be bound over to superior court. After the information is filed, the defendant appears for arraignment, at which time issues regarding bail and counsel are addressed (if they have not been previously), and a trial date is set. The superior court receives few "certified pleas" (cases in which a guilty plea was accepted in municipal court, and defendants are transferred to superior court for sentencing). All jury trials are held in Salinas.

PROSECUTOR'S OFFICE. The prosecutor is elected to a four-year term. There are 26 attorneys, with 12 of them assigned to felony cases. New attorneys are hired from private law practice, military judge advocates group, and directly from law school. Most of the attorneys have been in the office for five years, with some having 20 years of service. Training for new attorneys is offered through the California District Attorneys' Association (CDAA). Continuing training consists of scheduled in-office lectures, field trips, videotape sessions, and special courses offered by CDAA and the National Association of District Attorneys when funds are available.

The screening of felony cases is done by a senior district attorney who reviews the police report and decides whether to file, to reject, or to return the case to the police for further work. At the preliminary hearing, the assistant district attorney makes the final decision, after group discussion, whether to proceed or to abandon the case.

Globe

ENVIRONMENT. Gila County is a large geographic area (4,752 square miles), approximately half the size of Rhode Island. It is located approximately 90 miles east of Phoenix in the state's copper-mining region. It also includes a growing recreational and retirement community (Payson-Pine), although the Globe community is larger. Demographically, Gila County is a community of 37,000 persons, with 15 percent of the population identified as nonwhite (primarily Hispanic and American Indian as the county is bordered on the east by two Indian reservations). The per capita income in 1985 was $7,399.

COURT. Gila County Superior Court is a general jurisdiction trial court with two permanent judges with chambers in Globe and a commissioner in Payson. The current chief judge was appointed by the governor to the court in 1979, and the other judge was elected to the bench in 1987 after having been the county attorney and a contract defense attorney.

The Gila County Superior Courthouse is located in Globe, which is at the southeastern corner of the county, and there is a branch court located in Payson, which is in the northwestern quadrant. Two thirds of the cases are heard in Globe, and one third were heard in Payson. One of the indigent defense attorneys practices almost exclusively in Payson; the other attorneys occasionally practice there.

Within 24 hours after arrest for a felony offense, the defendant first appears in the limited jurisdiction justice court before a justice of the peace. This practice is followed regardless of where in the county the defendant is arrested. At the first appearance, a determination is made as to whether the defendant needs counsel. After the first appearance, the process becomes a bit different in the two locations. In Payson, the next proceeding is a preliminary hearing in the justice court. This hearing occurs approximately ten days after arrest for those in custody and later if the defendant is out on bond. The next proceeding is arraignment before a superior court commissioner. The commissioner can take pleas, hear motions, and sentence individuals. However, if jury trials are conducted, those proceedings are held in Globe by one of the superior court judges. If the first appearance is held in Globe, then the next proceeding is a hearing before a grand jury. Indigent defendants are then arraigned in superior court.

PROSECUTOR'S OFFICE. The county attorney is elected and directs a five-person professional staff, one of whom is part-time and one on contract. The prosecutors generally do not specialize, but one handles most of the DUI cases, and one handles most of the sexual and child abuse cases.

New attorneys are asked for a two-year commitment. The county attorney believes that it is difficult to recruit new attorneys (because of low salaries) and that it is difficult to keep them because of other opportunities (metropolitan county attorneys' offices, attorney general's office, and U.S. Attorney's Office). In 1989, for example, two of three full-time assistant county attorneys were admitted to the bar in 1988. The most senior assistant county attorney had been in practice for eight years and had been with the office for six years.

New attorneys begin first with misdemeanors, then move on to misdemeanor trials, and finally to felonies. Within the felony category, the county attorney screens cases for their degrees of seriousness.

Oxford

ENVIRONMENT. The population of Oxford County was 50,200 in 1986, approximately 4 percent of Maine's total population of 1,250,000. Oxford County is located in the southwestern mountain region of Maine. The basic industries in this area center on lumbering and paper production. The per capita income is $8,379, with just under 13 percent of the population living below the poverty level. Less than one-half of 1 percent of Oxford County is identified as nonwhite. The serious crime rate for Oxford was 1,781 index crimes per 100,00 population in 1985.

COURT. The Oxford County court system has two tiers: a superior court of general jurisdiction and two district courts of limited jurisdiction. The superior court courthouse is located in South Paris directly next to one of the district courts. The other district court is located in Rumford, which is the largest community in the county.

There are approximately 16 justices of the superior court who are appointed by the governor of the state for seven-year terms. These judges rotate through the 16 counties in Maine. Schedules are issued either every other month or every third month. However, judges may rotate to a different county each month, or they may stay in a single county for as long as three times in a month. The chief justice of the superior court assigns the justices; however, the regional court administrators are usually delegated much of this responsibility.

In the Oxford County Superior Court, one visiting judge usually hears cases for two to three weeks out of any given month. Criminal cases are usually given priority over civil cases. During the remaining days of the month, the judge usually rotates to Franklin County to hear cases. The superior court in Oxford does not usually conduct hearings during the months of July and August because the one available courtroom lacks air conditioning. The regional court administrator usually assigns one judge to handle cases in Oxford for the entire four weeks of the months of June and September.

There are three methods in which a criminal case can reach the Oxford County Superior Court. Approximately 40 percent of the cases are felonies that reach the superior court through grand jury indictments. Grand juries meet in Oxford approximately every three to four months. If an indictment is filed on a felony, an arraignment in superior court follows anywhere from a week to a month later. At arraignment, counsel is assigned, the indictment is read, and a plea is requested. It is at this stage that the defendant's attorney receives all the information that the prosecution has on the case. After a plea of not guilty, 21 days are allowed for filing motions. After this period, the trial is scheduled. There is usually a two-to-three-month wait for a scheduled trial date. Most pleas in Oxford County occur on the day of trial or at a motion hearing. The judge who takes the plea handles the sentencing. Sentencing usually occurs on the same day as the plea offering; murder and sex-related offenses may take a few months longer for the completion of tests and reports needed for sentencing.

The second method in which a case can reach the Oxford County Superior Court is to be transferred from the district court. Approximately 10 percent of the cases reach the superior court this way. These cases consist of misdemeanors in which a jury trial was requested.

The final method in which a case can reach the superior court is through a felony bindover. Forty percent of the cases reach the superior court in this manner. After an arrest on a felony charge, the defendant appears before a bail commissioner. If the defendant does not make bail, the first appearance before a district court judge is set within 24 hours. At the first appearance, defendants are advised of their rights, bail is reviewed, and indigency is determined, based on information concerning the defendant's income and assets. After the district court judge determines at the first appearance whether the defendant is indigent, the criminal case deputy clerk subsequently telephones an attorney to see if he or she will accept a court appointment. Finally, at the first appearance, the date for the probable cause hearing is set. For defendants released on bail, the hearing is scheduled six weeks later. For detained defendants, the hearing is set three weeks later. If the defendant is bound over at the probable cause hearing, then the case will take the same path in the superior court as those that were initiated by a direct indictment of a grand jury.

PROSECUTOR'S OFFICE. The prosecutor is an elected official who handles all cases except homicides in the three counties of Franklin, Oxford, and Androscoggin. In homicide cases, the attorney general represents the state. There are five assistant prosecutors, each of whom have been working there for at least five years. One assistant prosecutor is permanently stationed in South Paris.

Horizontal case management is the norm for criminal cases. A sexual abuse case may be handled by the same prosecutor throughout all stages of its development; however, this is not necessarily the norm for other cases. Training consists of attendance at annual, in-state programs for Maine's prosecutors. These programs provide updates on case law, procedures, and legislation. However, there is no ongoing training.

Island and San Juan

ENVIRONMENT. Island and San Juan counties are adjacent counties that consist only of islands. By western United States standards they are very small (212 square miles for Island; 179 square miles for San Juan). Both counties are rural in character; however, a naval air station gives Island County a somewhat different flavor. Both counties have low to virtually nonexistent minority populations and high real estate values. The median value of homes in San Juan county is $87,300—

the highest in the state and nearly one-third higher than the state median—and the median real estate value in Island County is nearly identical to the state median of $60,700. Crime rates are 2,278 and 2,843 per 100,000 population for Island and San Juan, respectively.

Island is the larger and less remote county with a population of 49,600 distributed between Whidby Island and Camano Island. Its population centers are about 90 minutes from Seattle. These are the towns of Oak Harbor, where the Whidby Island Naval Air Station is located, and Coupeville, the county seat.

San Juan County (population 9,200 in 1986) consists of four island population centers and several smaller islands with fewer than 100 year round residents. The four major islands—San Juan, Orcas, Lopez and Shaw—have state ferry service from Skagit County, 90 minutes north of Seattle by automobile. The ferry ride is 70 minutes to 2 hours, depending on stops. Tourist traffic on these ferries is constant, and in the peak summer season, the actual population of the islands swells by a factor of three to four. There is one incorporated town, Friday Harbor, which is the county seat.

COURT. Washington State has a two-tiered trial court—the general jurisdiction superior court and the limited jurisdiction district court. Felonies are filed in the superior court exclusively. The superior court holds sessions in each county, but judges in Washington may be elected to a judicial district that encompasses more than one county. This is the case with Island and San Juan counties. They are part of the Island judicial district. Judges run for election every four years on a nonpartisan ballot.

Charging is by information, although grand juries and a special proceeding called a "special inquiry judge" are authorized in statute. The latter is only occasionally used by the prosecutor, and grand juries also are rare. After arrest, if a defendant is in custody, there is a first appearance (bond hearing) within 24 hours, and an information must be filed in superior court within 72 hours (excluding weekends and holidays). In San Juan County, if a superior court judge is not available, a local lawyer sits as judge pro tem for the bond hearing. Arraignment is held promptly following the filing of the information (within a few weeks at the most); in San Juan County, the arraignment often will be held on the same day as the filing of the information, as a matter of scheduling convenience. Only in rare cases will there be a plea at arraignment. The arraignment hearing is the time for appointment of counsel. A second hearing is set at arraignment for about two to three weeks—for early guilty pleas, pretrial matters, and trial scheduling. These proceedings often will be continued at least once.

PROSECUTOR'S OFFICE. The prosecuting attorney in Washington State is elected every four years. In these small counties, there are no in-house training programs. Prosecuting attorneys attend training sessions made available through the

Washington Association of Prosecuting Attorneys (WAPA), the bar association, and other state and local training forums. They are allowed a travel allowance for one county-funded educational program each year, and other training is fitted in on an "as available" basis. The WAPA services for prosecuting attorneys (newsletters, technical assistance, and so forth) are highly developed, however, and assistant prosecuting attorneys also network with colleagues in other counties.

ISLAND COUNTY PROSECUTOR. There are five attorneys in addition to the elected prosecutor. One senior attorney handles felony cases with the help of a deputy whose primary responsibility is juvenile matters. New attorneys start at $28 to 30,000 per year. Attorneys tend to stay five or more years, if they last more than a year or so at the entry-level position.

SAN JUAN COUNTY PROSECUTOR. The prosecutor in San Juan County has a six-year tenure and will seek office again. The elected prosecutor in San Juan County is expected to be personally involved in the county's civil (primarily land use) matters, and his background is in land use law. He delegates responsibility for the criminal caseload to the deputy prosecutor. At election time, the prosecutor's attitudes on the subject of environmental law will be probed far more deeply than his views on criminal justice.

The office is staffed by the elected prosecutor, one full-time assistant prosecutor, and one part-time assistant. The assistant prosecutor handles the criminal caseload. From 1980 to 1990, three individuals have held the criminal assistant attorney position. The salary of the current criminal assistant attorney (in his third year) is $34,000. The philosophy and quality of criminal prosecution during the past ten years has tended to reflect the experience and attitudes of the assistant prosecuting attorneys.